GREEN WITCHCRAFT
FOR BEGINNERS

A Guide to the Magic of Nature, with Seasonal and Elemental Magic, Herbs, Flowers, Crystals, Divination, Plus Spells and Rituals for the Green Witch and Wiccans

LISA CHAMBERLAIN

Green Witchcraft for Beginners

Copyright © 2023 by Lisa Chamberlain.

All rights reserved. No part of this book may be reproduced in any form without permission in writing from the author. Reviewers may quote brief passages in reviews

Published by **Chamberlain Publications**

ISBN-13: 978-1-912715-84-8

Disclaimer

No part of this publication may be reproduced or transmitted in any form or by any means, mechanical or electronic, including photocopying or recording, or by any information storage and retrieval system, or transmitted by email without permission in writing from the publisher.

While all attempts have been made to verify the information provided in this publication, neither the author nor the publisher assumes any responsibility for errors, omissions, or contrary interpretations of the subject matter herein.

This book is for entertainment purposes only. The views expressed are those of the author alone, and should not be taken as expert instruction or commands. The reader is responsible for his or her own actions.

Adherence to all applicable laws and regulations, including international, federal, state, and local governing professional licensing, business practices, advertising, and all other aspects of doing business in the US, Canada, or any other jurisdiction is the sole responsibility of the purchaser or reader.

Neither the author nor the publisher assumes any responsibility or liability whatsoever on the behalf of the purchaser or reader of these materials.

Any perceived slight of any individual or organization is purely unintentional.

YOUR FREE GIFT

Thank you for adding this book to your Wiccan library! To learn more, why not join Lisa's Wiccan community and get an exclusive, free spell book?

The book is a great starting point for anyone looking to try their hand at practicing magic. The ten beginner-friendly spells can help you to create a positive atmosphere within your home, protect yourself from negativity, and attract love, health, and prosperity.

Little Book of Spells is now available to read on your laptop, phone, tablet, Kindle or Nook device!

To download, simply visit the following link:

www.wiccaliving.com/bonus

GET THREE FREE AUDIOBOOKS FROM LISA CHAMBERLAIN

Did you know that all of Lisa's books are available in audiobook format? Best of all, you can get **three audiobooks completely free** as part of a 30-day trial with Audible.

Wicca Starter Kit contains three of Lisa's most popular books for beginning Wiccans, all in one convenient place. It's the best and easiest way to learn more about Wicca while also taking audiobooks for a spin! Simply visit:

www.wiccaliving.com/free-wiccan-audiobooks

Alternatively, *Spellbook Starter Kit* is the ideal option for building your magical repertoire using candle and color magic, crystals and mineral stones, and magical herbs. Three spellbooks —over 150 spells—are available in one free volume, here:

www.wiccaliving.com/free-spell-audiobooks

Audible members receive free audiobooks every month, as well as exclusive discounts. It's a great way to experiment and see if audiobook learning works for you.

If you're not satisfied, you can cancel anytime within the trial period. You won't be charged, and you can still keep your books!

CONTENTS

Introduction 10

Chapter One: Walking the Green Path 13

    What is Green Witchcraft? 14
    Interweaving Paths 17
    Ancestors of the Green Witch 20
    Magical Stewards of the Earth 23
    Warning: It's Not Easy Being Green 26
    A Barefoot Grounding Ritual 28

Chapter Two: Nature and Divine Intelligence 30

    A Magical Partnership 31
    Plant Intelligence 32
    The Magic of Animals 36
    Intention and Abundance 38
    The Rhythm of the Cosmos 40
        The Sun and Moon 40
        The Planets and the Zodiac 43
    Shadow Work, Divine Intelligence, and Magical Goals 45
        The Wisdom of the Forest 46

Chapter Three: Elemental Magic 48

    The Core Energies of Nature 49
    The Elements and Green Magic 52
        Elemental Qualities and Magical Goals 54

The Elements and Spiritual Alchemy	*57*
Elemental Balance Spell	61
Elemental Correspondences	64

Chapter Four: Seasonal and Lunar Magic 66

Life, Death, and Rebirth	67
Seasonal Energies	70
Winter	*71*
Spring	*72*
Summer	*73*
Autumn	*74*
Lunar Seasons	76
The Magic of Change	79
Winter Dream Spell	*80*
Spring Seed Intention Spell	*81*
Summer Fire Ritual	*82*
Autumn Clearing-Out Ritual	*83*

Chapter Five: Green Divination 84

Nature is Talking to You	85
Elemental Communication	87
Animal Messengers	90
Open Your Channel to Nature's Wisdom	93

Chapter Six: Plants and the Green Witch 95

The Magical Plant Kingdom	96
Gathering Plants in the Wild	100
Harmonious Harvesting	*101*
The Green Witch's Garden	103
Magical Herbs and Flowers for Pots and Planters	*103*
Magical Herbs	*104*

Magical Flowers *107*
Magical Gardening Tips *109*
Drying and Storing Herbs *111*
Gardening with the Moon 114

Chapter Seven: Creating Sacred Space 116

Harmonize Your Living Space with Nature's Energies . 117
Magical Plant Companions 119
"Green Thumb" Advice for House Plants *122*
Crystals: Bringing Earth Energies into Your Home 124
Clearing and Blessing Your Sacred Space 128

Chapter Eight: Spells, Recipes, and Magical Inspirations 130

Practical Magic for the Green Witch 131
Energize Your Magical Allies *131*
Tree Magic *132*
Nature's Bounty Abundance Jar *134*
Charm for Adapting to Change *136*
Crystals for Gardens and Houseplants *138*
The Magic of Tea *139*
Essential Oil Allies *141*
Natural Magical Incense *143*
Magical Associations of Common Herbs *145*
Magical Associations of Common Wildflowers *146*
Magical Associations of Common Trees *147*
Magical Associations of Crystals and Stones *148*
Magical Associations of Essential Oils *149*
Magical Associations of Incense *150*

Conclusion 151

Suggestions for Further Reading *153*

INTRODUCTION

Like many witches, I was blessed enough to be raised in a home surrounded by nature. My earliest memories are of watching seagulls glide over the waters of the glacial lake in our back yard. I grew up running through the woods, making boats from bark and racing them down creeks, and wandering through fields of wildflowers. At a very young age, I communicated with nature spirits and other beings on the invisible plane when I was outdoors. (My mother called them my "imaginary friends," but these beings definitely came from outside my imagination!)

Although I was not raised as a witch, and didn't discover magic or witchcraft until I was a young adult, those early experiences infused me with a love of nature that primed me for embracing the green path. The term "green witchcraft" wasn't widely in use during the early days of my spiritual explorations, but it was the emphasis on nature that drew me to Wicca, more than any other aspect, so it was only natural (pun intended) that I would gravitate toward this kindred path as well, as part of my eclectic practice.

Perhaps you have similar stories of connecting with nature as a child. Or perhaps you've always been an urban dweller who is drawn to being in nature. Whatever your background, the fact that you're reading this book suggests an affinity with the natural world and a call to explore its spiritual dimensions through the path of green witchcraft. And whether you're new to working magic or an old hand at spellcasting, you're likely interested in finding new ideas and inspiration for your practice.

The first thing to know about green witchcraft is that there's no actual definition for green witchcraft. It's a path within the wider witching world, but it has as many possible descriptions as the number of people who call themselves green witches. That said, there are several areas of focus that can be said to comprise the green path, with plenty of room for overlap with other paths, such as Wicca, and infinite room for eclectic innovations.

This guide begins with an orientation to the core aspects of green witchcraft, as well as the historical contexts from which it has emerged. We'll examine "green" philosophy, including living in balance with the needs of the Earth, how divine intelligence is expressed through nature in all of its manifestations, and the benefits of co-creating with this intelligence for a more harmonious life. We'll look at the role of the elements, the energies of the seasons, the magic of the lunar phases, and the ongoing cycles of life, death, and rebirth that keep all of existence going.

There's a practical focus as well, with exercises and advice for grounding and balancing your energy; receiving intuitive messages, signs and signals from nature; working with your shadow; and establishing energetically balanced sacred space. Of course, there's also plenty of information about plants—in the wild, in the garden, and in the house—and various other spells, rituals, recipes, and ideas for incorporating nature in your practice.

This introductory book is intended as a starting-off point in your exploration of the green path. As always, I encourage you to read more about any aspect that your heart calls you toward. May the information you find here inspire you on your journey.

CHAPTER ONE
WALKING THE GREEN PATH

WHAT IS GREEN WITCHCRAFT?

When it comes to witchcraft, terminology and definitions are often pretty slippery. One person's idea of what "witchcraft" is might look very different from someone else's. There were times in history when simply knowing about herbs and healing remedies was enough to get a person labeled as a witch. And in recent decades, there have been plenty of raging arguments about just how "witchy" one needs to look and behave in order to deserve the designation.

To complicate things further, the word "green" is often used these days as a sort of marketing shorthand for products or policies that contribute to a healthy and sustainable environment for humanity and the planet as a whole. But since an appreciation for nature is already more or less built into much of modern witchcraft, what is it that makes a green witch "green," as opposed to simply a witch?

There's no easy answer to this question, since green witchcraft is not a religion, or even a long-established tradition of witchcraft. The term is really just a modern framing for an ageless way of being, of working with the energies and rhythms of the natural world.

But there's no set of agreed-upon instructions, rules, beliefs, or standard practices that clearly defines what green witchcraft is or isn't. Every green witch will likely describe their path somewhat differently, as every human being has a unique experience of their spiritual connection to nature. That said, there are a few common characteristics that most green witches would probably agree are core aspects of this path.

The central focus of green witchcraft is on working with the magical energetic properties of everything that grows in the ground—trees, herbs, flowers, and other plants. These energies can be used in healing, divination, and other magic. Indeed, there is a very heavy emphasis on all things plant-related: growing, harvesting, and working with herbs in both healing and spellwork.

Green witches tend to be gardeners, foragers, or both. They are likely to be skilled in making potions, tinctures, teas, oils, and other remedies for physical, emotional, and magical needs. Depending on the witch, the focus may be more on crafting these remedies for physical use, or they may lean primarily in the direction of spells and charms. For most green witches, it's a blend of both. In other words, basic herbal knowledge is part of the path, but typically isn't the only goal of one's practice.

If you are just starting out along this path, don't be discouraged or intimidated by these words. You don't really have to have a garden or have access to wild plants to be a green witch. You can live in an apartment building with some houseplants and a few potted herbs on the windowsill. And you don't have to be an expert herbalist. This knowledge comes with experience and experimentation, which is all part of the path. Even the most experienced green witches (or witches of any path, really) will tell you that there is always more to learn.

Green witchcraft is not solely focused on the plant kingdom, however. We also work with other aspects of nature, including crystals and stones, fossils and feathers, sand and seashells, and sacred outdoor space in general, wherever we find it.

Green witches generally cultivate an understanding of and a working relationship with the elements found within all of nature: earth, air, water, and fire. Some may also engage in weather magic, or working with the energies of particular weather phenomena such as thunderstorms, blizzards, or even heatwaves. As with other forms of witchcraft, there is also an aspect of honoring the changes of the seasons, the phases of the moon, and the life/death/rebirth cycles found throughout the experience of life on Earth.

Many green witches also work with a diverse array of nature spirits and multidimensional beings typically referred to as "faeries." This may take the form of leaving offerings for the spirits they sense on the land around them or in favorite outdoor spaces. Some may request the assistance of faeries in magical workings, or simply in protecting their gardens and helping them to thrive.

For some green witches, a relationship with the Fae is an integral part of the path, while for others, it may not be much of a focus at all. However, it's worth noting that in ancient British and Celtic lore, the color green was very much associated with faeries, who were often said to be wearing green. For this reason, many witches who work with the Fae consider themselves to be on the green path.

INTERWEAVING PATHS

It's important to note that other, related paths within the wider world of witchcraft may also play a role in the green witch's practice. Kitchen witchery, for example, is a common overlapping path that is a fairly logical extension of green witchcraft. After all, if you're growing culinary herbs in your magical garden, it only makes sense to utilize them in a magical meal! In fact, brewing magical teas is a pretty common staple in all kinds of witchcraft, and can certainly be considered both a "green" and "kitchen" witchcraft practice.

One path of witchcraft that is often compared to and distinguished from green witchcraft is hedge witchcraft. The hedge witch is also a friend to nature, plants, and sacred outdoor space. But the focus of hedge witchcraft is more on taking spiritual journeys to the nonphysical realms, often referred to collectively as the Otherworld.

These journeys often (but not always) involve the use of specific plant allies in the form of teas, tinctures, ointments, and incense. Hedge witches travel to the Otherworld to gain information and insight from the spirit realms. By contrast, green witches are typically more focused on the physical realm, working with the Earth to bring about material changes in their lives through healing and spellwork.

This doesn't mean, however, that green witches don't interact with the spirit realms or experience multiple planes of reality while they are working at their craft. Green witches may indeed have a little (or a lot) of the hedge witch in them. For example, they may choose the most effective herbs to use for a particular purpose, by listening for instructions from the spirit world, or from the plants themselves. And while there is a conventional distinction between working with the natural world and journeying into the realm of the "supernatural," in reality everything is a co-creation of the entire universe. In other words, it's really all "natural" on both sides of the veil between physical and nonphysical reality.

It's also important to note that plenty of witches who *don't* call themselves "green" still revere nature, work with herbs, and may even be skilled gardeners. This includes Wiccans, of course, whose cosmology revolves around the cyclical seasonal patterns of the Wheel of the Year, and can also apply to practitioners of British Traditional Witchcraft (BTW) and other lesser-known traditional paths.

In fact, there are plenty of witches who identify as Green Wiccans, whose worship of the Goddess and the God is focused on divine archetypes like Gaia, the Earth Mother, and Pan, a quintessential nature god. However, as stated earlier, green witchcraft is not a religion and isn't in itself concerned with deity. If asked, a green witch might say that their connection with "deity," or the divine, comes from striving to live in harmony and balance with nature as a whole, and that their magical power is accessed from that harmonious state.

Likewise, green witchcraft doesn't necessarily involve the ceremonial-style magic and ritual found in Wicca and other

BTW-style paths. The ritual format of Wicca, for example, with its traditional tools and altar placements, may or may not be part of an individual's spiritual practice. Green witches do engage in ritual, but it's just as likely to be a free-form, inspired-on-the-spot kind of activity as a formal, scripted, regularly practiced ritual.

When it comes to ritual "tools," a green witch might work with items from the natural world—a branch of driftwood for a wand, an upturned seashell for a bowl or cup, and so on. But these objects are seen more as *allies* or *partners* in magical co-creation, with their own inherent intelligence, than as "implements" to be employed by the practitioner.

As for magic, the emphasis is typically on practical work like crafting teas, balms, and herbal charm bags, again using natural ingredients. Some may even avoid using manufactured spell ingredients like glitter or glue, synthetic oils, or ribbons, for example. Again, there are no hard and fast rules here. The path of the green witch is defined differently by everyone who is drawn to walk it. It's a path marked by the mysteries and wonders of nature, but it's up to each practitioner to say what it means, for them, to be a green witch.

ANCESTORS OF THE GREEN WITCH

Unlike Wicca and other established paths, there's no documented history of the origins of green witchcraft. However, many beliefs and practices that can be classified as "green" have existed in one form or another for centuries, stemming back to a time when most of humanity lived very close to the Earth, aware of their dependence on the cycles of nature for their survival.

Yet the people we think of as our spiritual ancestors would not likely have identified themselves as "witches," at least not by the 16th century, when modern English came into use. The Old English word *wicca* ("sorcerer" or "diviner") may be the inspiration for our modern concept of "witch," but by the 1500s, widespread persecution of "witches" was well underway, so it was not a term that anyone wanted to be known by.

A more accurate term for the green witches of the past would be "folk healers." In the days before conventional medicine and family doctors, people would bring their medical issues to the folk healers in their communities. These practitioners were skilled herbalists as well as shamans and seers, who often used magic and divination as part of their healing techniques. You could almost think of them as the "holistic" healers of their time, going beyond the physical or biological level and into the spiritual realms in order to identify and solve the underlying problems of their clients.

Folk healers might also provide a variety of non-medical services to their communities, including love charms and potions, divination, locating lost items, hex removal, and other magical remedies. These practitioners had different names in different areas of Europe. They were called *benandanti* in Italy ("good walkers") and *klok gumma* or *klok gubbe* in Swedish ("wise old woman" or "wise old man"). In England, they were called "cunning folk."

Records dating back to at least the 15th century show folk healers operating throughout Europe, with each country, region, and even county having their own specific folklore traditions. In fact, indigenous cultures all around the world have their own version of a "folk healer," from the *curanderos* of Central and South America to the shamans of Mongolia to the Ngangkari of Australia.

From the 17th century onward, the evolution of modern science created a distinct split between medicine and magic in the Western world. Scholars and scientists emphasized objective observation, empiricism, reason, and logic over intuition, mysticism, and spirit communication. Medicine became a discipline rooted in objective reality, while magic (which was basically anything that evidence-based science couldn't explain) was relegated to the realm of superstition and fantasy. Eventually, folk healers became largely a thing of the past.

This divergence between magic and healing ultimately led to amazing and life-saving discoveries in the medical field. Yet because modern science focuses solely on the physical plane, leaving non-physical reality out of the equation, it also created a false construct of the body as separate from the mind and spirit, which many holistic healers believe omits crucial information from our overall understanding of health. Modern medicine also favored synthetic pharmaceutical treatments over natural herbs, which over time caused an erosion of our collective knowledge of herbal remedies.

At the same time, the industrial revolution and the rapid urbanization that followed made it possible for large communities to live at a much further remove from the natural world than our ancestors would ever have dreamed possible. In fact, some people live their entire lives with little to no understanding of how their food is grown or where it comes from.

Theoretically, you could spend your life in a comfortable, climate-controlled environment, order everything you need online, and never leave your house. Of course, this disconnection between people and nature has created an imbalance with the Earth we live on, polluting the land, air, and water that we still need in order to survive.

It's in this context that green witchcraft has emerged as a modern form of an ancient spirituality, and its increasing popularity suggests that more and more people are seeking a new pathway back to living in harmony with the Earth. Green witchcraft could be considered a revival of ancient approaches to magic, healing, and divine connection, adapted for modern times.

MAGICAL STEWARDS OF THE EARTH

Many green witches see themselves as both partners and stewards of the earth, and strive to live in harmony with nature's best interests as part of their practice. The earth is the abundant source of all the physical materials we work magic with, as well as the food that sustains us and helps us thrive. So, it simply makes practical sense to take care of it as best we can. And as a bonus, as you will learn if you walk this path, magic gets more powerful when you work in harmony with the Earth and its inhabitants.

This means, for example, that a green witch is typically not going to use chemical cleaning products, herbicides, or pesticides. Instead, products made from natural ingredients are the ideal. Many cleaning agents can be made with essential oils, vinegar, and baking soda, and green witches often like to create their own magically charged solutions, integrating the act of cleaning with a magical intention like protection for the home or infusing the kitchen with peaceful and joyful vibrations.

Likewise, a green witch's personal care products, such as lotion, toothpaste, soap, shaving cream, etc. tend to be natural as opposed to synthetic. Plenty of DIY beauty products like facial masks and body fragrances can be whipped up at home and magically charged as well. A green witch will opt for natural fabrics in clothing and household linens, and choose organic, environmentally conscious foods when possible. Buying in bulk and limiting the use of disposable items are also great ways to live in harmony with the Earth. If you have the ability, composting food scraps helps reduce waste and provides free nutrients for potted plants and magical gardens alike.

In fact, soil health is an important but often overlooked issue when it comes to the environment and the quality of our food supply. The green witch blessed with a yard or garden will avoid using chemicals to deal with weeds and pests, and work instead in harmony with the ecosystem. This might include using compost and natural soil amendments, choosing natural pesticides to preserve plants while protecting pollinators, and planting cover crops. These are approaches aligned with the holistic and science-based movement of permaculture, which advocates working *with* nature, rather than against it, in order to allow nature's inherent divine intelligence to work its magic under the surface of the soil.

As we will see in Chapter 2, permaculture-inspired strategies, such as regenerative farming, can result in more robust and healthy abundance than conventional approaches that use chemicals to try to control nature. Although permaculture is not a spiritual movement per se, it is very much aligned with the green witch ethic. Anyone interested in magical gardening or landscaping would do well to learn more about this philosophy and the benefits of putting it into practice in their own corner of the world.

Of course, there can be circumstances when more toxic substances are needed, such as discovering an active wasp nest in the immediate vicinity of your front door. People can certainly be forgiven for looking out for their own safety in such a circumstance! But green witches will still strive to do the least possible harm at all times, and take measures to prevent the need to rely on harmful chemicals in the future. For example, you might purchase wasp nest decoys to hang in places where you want to avoid those feisty stinging pollinators.

Speaking of insects, these are usually the hardest aspect of nature for people to fully embrace—even for aspiring witches. If you have instinctual negative reactions to "bugs" of all kinds, try learning more about their roles in the ecosystem, and seeing them as important contributors to the natural world. Bugs are a great illustration of the Law of Attraction at work in your life—the more you fear or hate them, the more you tend to attract them to you, so try to lower your emotional resistance to these tiny creatures.

Avoid killing insects unless it's truly necessary. You don't have to let yourself be eaten alive by mosquitoes, but try rescuing harmless insects that make their way into your home rather than squashing them. If you can soften your emotional reactions to bugs, you'll stop noticing them so much and they'll leave you alone more of the time. This will make it easier for you to feel and commune with the magical energies of nature.

WARNING: IT'S NOT EASY BEING GREEN

Although green witches love to work with nature, it's important to acknowledge that nature is not always kind or safe. Death is very much part of our overall ecosystem. Living beings are eaten by other beings, forests are kept healthy through natural fire cycles, and hail can destroy a season's crops in ten minutes. Very few humans alive today in the civilized world could survive for long in the wild. Nature is divine, but that doesn't mean it's easy to live with, or that you don't need to keep your wits about you.

This is especially true of the plant kingdom. Many plants have healing properties, while other plants can make us ill, cause horrible rashes, and even kill us. And just to keep things interesting, some plants can both heal and kill, depending on how they're used. This is why *no one, witch or otherwise, should under any circumstances use an herb they are unfamiliar with for any purpose.*

Even if you've already developed an excellent sixth-sense connection to the natural world, always research everything you plan to work with. Hunches and inklings are great, but they're no substitute for tried-and-true knowledge. In fact, looking up your potential herb (or flower, or essential oil) of choice will actually help you strengthen your intuitive relationship with nature, as you'll be able to get confirmation that your hunch was on target.

Also note that none of the information in this book is meant to be taken as medical advice, or as a substitute for consulting a licensed medical practitioner. While it's safe enough to use some magical herbs in certain simple remedies for physical ailments, such as drinking chamomile tea to reduce anxiety, herbs are complex substances that require specialized knowledge to be used safely and effectively for most medical issues—especially serious ones.

If you are pregnant, take pharmaceutical medications, or have any serious conditions, it is imperative that you research possible drug interactions or other complications before using herbs topically or internally. Consult your family physician or a licensed herbalist if you have access to one.

A BAREFOOT GROUNDING RITUAL

One way to avoid making unpleasant mistakes when working with nature, and with working magic of any kind, is to make sure you're grounded and focused before you begin. Grounding is a means of connecting your energy to the earth, and has positive effects on mental, physical, and spiritual health. For witches, grounding facilitates a calm, centered state where you are best able to harness your own personal power. This practice also helps the energy you interact with in magical work flow through you at a comfortable rate.

There are many ways to ground your energy. You can use meditation, breathing techniques, journaling, yoga, qigong, and other methods to bring yourself into a grounded and focused state. One simple, yet effective way to ground is to place your bare feet on the earth itself. This can be done on grass, soil, or sand (and if you're up for the mess, mud is quite delightful!) You can stand or sit, but sitting is recommended for trying the following method.

- Bring a chair or a blanket to sit on, and place your feet firmly on the earth. (If you're sitting on a blanket, you might try keeping your hands planted on the ground as well.)

- As you begin the ritual, simply observe how you feel. Notice any sensations in your body and your general state of mind.

- Now close your eyes and take three deep breaths. Visualize any unwanted energy in your physical body or your mind being absorbed gently into the earth.

- As you begin to feel lighter, with a quieter mind, visualize a column of green light flowing upward from the ground into the soles of your feet. See the light climb up through your body and into your heart center, then slowly spreading throughout the rest of your body.

- Sit this way for 15-30 minutes. (You can also journal if you like, which is a good option if you find it hard to sit still.)

- Before you get up, observe any changes in the energy of your body. Do you feel calmer? More enlivened? What shifts do you feel taking place?

- Close the ritual with some words of gratitude for the healing energy of the earth, and set the intention to carry this feeling of groundedness with you for rest of your day.

Note: this visualization can also be done indoors. However, it's more powerful to use the energy of the earth directly. A quality grounding mat is highly recommended, as these draw earth energy through a grounded electrical outlet, and have been shown to have all kinds of health benefits with regular use.

CHAPTER TWO
NATURE AND DIVINE INTELLIGENCE

A MAGICAL PARTNERSHIP

Nature was the original source of mystery and magic. For our ancestors, everything in the natural world—the glittering stars, the unfolding of a flower, the emergence of a giant tree out of a tiny seed—reflected a spiritual intelligence beyond human understanding.

As our scientific knowledge of the natural world has evolved over the centuries, it's become clear that nature truly is an intelligent, self-sustaining system. While nature can manifest in ways that seem chaotic from our perspective, it is actually functioning in perfect order, if left undisturbed. What's more, nature is always working to resolve imbalances caused by human activity, though it often needs our participation to come back fully into balance.

For the witch on the green path, it's helpful to understand nature as a physical embodiment of partnership with spirit, or divine intelligence. This intelligence can be found in all of existence, and is at the heart of what we tap into when we work magic. Learning from nature is an important part of understanding green magic, and it's also a first step toward participating in the healing of the Earth.

PLANT INTELLIGENCE

Plants are a central practical focus of green witchcraft, and are excellent teachers when it comes to divine intelligence. The ancient Greek philosopher Aristotle believed that plants have "psyches," a word normally used to describe the human attributes of soul, mind, or spirit. Many green witches speak about the spirit of plants, and even some modern scientists have described the inherent intelligence of plants as "consciousness." Regardless of the terminology, however, it's clear that these seemingly inert, mute inhabitants of nature have much more going on than meets the eye.

For one thing, plants have at least three times the number of distinct senses as human beings, which enable them to sense and respond to everything in their environments, including sounds, chemicals in the air, different wavelengths of light, and other plant life in their vicinity. Perhaps the most obvious example of this sensory capacity is the behavior of vines, which can detect nearby support structures and grow in their direction. But this intelligence also exists underground—the roots of plants can detect obstacles in their way and shift direction in order to avoid them.

Many experiments conducted on plants have shown surprising results. In one, a plant exposed to an audio recording of a caterpillar chewing on a leaf produced chemicals used to defend against predator attacks. In another, a researcher removed a cabbage plant from its pot and ripped it into pieces in the presence of a second cabbage plant, then left the room. The surviving plant was then connected to a polygraph machine, and several researchers entered the room, one at a time. The polygraph registered no physiological response to the presence of any of the researchers except for the "culprit" who had killed the first plant. Even more surprisingly, plants reacted to the researchers' mere *thoughts* of harming them, but only when the thought was coupled with the actual intention to do harm.

The idea that plants could be mind-readers may not be a huge leap to make for green witches who have discovered how sensitive plants can be to external stimuli such as music, or the energetic frequency of kind words spoken in the plants' presence. But these discoveries provide a fascinating glimpse into the interconnectedness of different species—in this case, humans and plants—in the divine web of creation.

A more complex example exists in forest ecosystems, where a "web" of fungi living underground facilitates "information exchange" across species. Scientists have tracked the flow of nutrients and chemical signals exchanged between trees along pathways within this web. Older trees will share nutrients with younger trees that are still too shaded to get sufficient sunlight, and trees of one species will actually trade vital nutrients back and forth with other species at different points in the growing season. This activity, invisible to human eyes, is a perfect illustration of the co-creational heart, or consciousness, of nature.

Divine intelligence can also be seen in your own backyard, where native and naturalized wild plants often show up uninvited among the carefully tended grass. Most people consider these "weeds" to be a nuisance, but they're actually helpful indicators of the type and quality of the soil they're found in. For example, crabgrass will crop up in poor soil that's low in calcium and high in chlorine. Dandelions grow in low-calcium soil that's high in potassium. People who want rich, green lawns can use soil amendments like organic matter and gypsum to create more grass-friendly soil that's less attractive to these "weeds." Understanding these plants as a means of communication from nature makes them partners in restoring healthy soil, rather than obstacles to a healthy-looking lawn.

What's more, plants can actually help balance the conditions of the soil they grow in. Dandelions have wide-spreading taproots that break up hard-packed soil and pull calcium from deeper underground, making it more available to other plants, including grass. Clover pulls nitrogen into the soil from the air, and also attracts earthworms, which are always good for soil. And if there are rabbits in the vicinity, clover is a good way to keep them satisfied enough to ignore your garden plants, at least for a while! Learning from and working with what shows up in your yard can help you rebalance the soil around your home. And of course, discovering the medicinal and magical uses of your "weeds" can be a great boost to your green witch education!

After all, witches draw on this very energy of natural intelligence when working magic with plants. Magical correspondences, such as those traditionally observed in

Western witchcraft, are really ways of describing the particular forms this intelligence takes in any given plant.

As you learn more about the plants in your corner of the world, you may find these correspondences helpful in interpreting the energies you feel from your plants. However, you may also pick up on different energies that don't necessarily align with traditional correspondences. If this is the case, always go with your gut. The communication between you and the plant is always more significant than any magical information you read in a book—including this one!

THE MAGIC OF ANIMALS

Animals are, of course, every bit as integral as plants to nature's brilliant design. One of the most exciting demonstrations of this is the reintroduction of wolves in Yellowstone National Park in 1995.

Wolves had been eliminated from the park in the early 20th century, resulting in an increased elk population that was out of balance with their available food supply. Elk expanded into greater areas of the park and ate the willow and aspen trees along the waterways, eliminating the winter food supply for the beaver population, which went into serious decline. The absence of beaver dams in the rivers and streams led to erosion along the banks, causing many plant species to also decline. Each of these losses caused further disruptions for other animals dependent on the affected species, from the lowly mouse to the lofty owl.

In the decades since wolves were reintroduced in the park, amazing changes have been documented. The elk population came down to sustainable numbers and stopped overgrazing the river banks, allowing the aspen and willow trees to recover. The trees brought back the beavers, and their dams helped the rivers hold their natural course, which reduced erosion. More stable soil along the banks allowed more plant life to thrive again, which brought more mice and rabbits and more of their predators, such as hawks, owls, and snakes.

Biologists assert that other factors, especially variations in climate, also contributed to some of these effects—nature is after all an extremely complex system. But from a magical perspective, these other cooperating factors were part of nature's divine, conscious response to the wolves' reintroduction. Nature co-creates with us through life forms and forces of all kinds, including the presence and behavior of animals. In Yellowstone, the animals showed us how actions taken for the betterment of nature can create beneficial and even astounding results.

Animals have always held spiritual significance for cultures around the world, through origin myths and symbolism, and their presence as omens or signs from the spiritual plane. Many green witches work with animals in a variety of ways.

Domestic animals living with witches may enjoy being present for ritual and magical workings—especially cats, who are especially sensitive to nonphysical energy! Bones, egg shells, and feathers may be part of spellwork, but only when found, and never as a result of harming an animal. A green witch may or may not work with specific animal guides in their practice, but animal sightings in waking life as well as in dreams can be read as messages from the higher realms. After all, animals are part of the divine language of natural intelligence, as we will see in Chapter 5.

INTENTION AND ABUNDANCE

Another wonderful example of co-creation with nature is demonstrated in the movie *The Biggest Little Farm*. This film shows how a small group of people used organic and regenerative farming techniques to transform an abandoned, arid, essentially unfarmable piece of land in drought-plagued southern California into a lush, biodiverse ecosystem that produces over 200 varieties of vegetables and fruits.

Their mission was to work with the interconnectedness of nature to rehabilitate the land and foster the growth cycles that are inherent to nature's design. They started by planting cover crops to return nutrients to the parched soil, which over time created an environment where many different forms of life could thrive.

The results were dramatically beneficial, but working in "harmony" with nature doesn't mean that nature always cooperates the way we'd like it to. As wildlife returned to the now-thriving land, unexpected problems had to be met with humane and organic solutions.

When slugs threatened their fruit trees, the farmers brought their ducks to the orchard to eat them. When coyotes were ravaging their chickens, they stationed a guard dog near the chicken coop, which drove the coyotes to hunt gophers instead. This was a bonus victory, as the gophers had been attacking the roots of their fruit trees.

The approaches used by these farmers are markedly different from those used in modern conventional agriculture, which has been responsible for extensive pollution and soil erosion over the past several decades. The decision to work in co-creation with nature, rather than domination over nature, led to solutions that work for humans and the ecosystem alike, ultimately bringing in more abundance and healthier, better-tasting food.

Today, the farm has expanded from 80 acres to over 230 acres in roughly ten years, with several areas on the land designated as Certified Wildlife Habitat. Their produce is sold at local farmers markets and grocery stores, and is featured on menus at several Los Angeles restaurants.

These farmers may not have practiced witchcraft, but they did work with the natural divine intelligence that drives magic, using positive intentions to guide their actions. Their philosophy for tending to the Earth is a great example of the green witch ethic, as well as an illustration of the Law of Return—what you put out into the world comes back to you. When you work with the intention for the benefit of all, there are greater rewards for all.

THE RHYTHM OF THE COSMOS

While the focus of green witchcraft is about the Earth, our home planet is obviously not the end-all-be-all when it comes to divine intelligence. There are also off-planet partners in the co-creation of our universe—celestial bodies holding various energies that manifest on both the physical and spiritual planes.

The stars and planets move through space in a predictable pattern that has been observed since ancient times, and as technology has evolved, so has our knowledge about these bodies, their movements, and their energetic influences. These include physical effects which can be observed scientifically, and emotional, psychological, and spiritual effects that are interpreted through the metaphysical discipline of astrology.

THE SUN AND MOON

The sun is the most obvious and essential co-creative partner in this cosmic dance, at least for the Earth and its inhabitants. The daylight patterns and seasonal cycles created by Earth's rotating orbit around the sun are what makes life and growth possible. The dark is just as necessary as the light, as everything that's alive needs periods of rest, including the soil.

Each species of plant, animal, and insect is suited to particular time spans of light and dark, warmth and cold. In climates with dramatic temperature shifts, the winter months make it possible to grow a wide variety of annual plants for food, especially vegetables, as these plants are designed to grow for a shorter period of time than the perennial fruits and culinary herbs of tropical lands. Taken altogether, the effects of the sun and the relative presence or absence of its light create a stunning diversity of foods to sustain us.

Humans also need the sun for optimal well-being. Our bodies create vitamin D when exposed to sunlight, which boosts immunity to illness and can help mitigate seasonal depression. Just as with plants and animals, not every person needs the same amount of sunlight, but we all need some amount of natural warmth and light in our lives.

As for the moon, while its effects on Earth-dwelling life may be more subtle, it definitely has its own pull, as anyone who's ever watched a tide come in can attest. With its own gravitational force, the moon affects the oceans as well as people, animals, and even plants.

Women's menstrual cycles are often in rhythm with the shifting moon phases, and a full moon can affect moods and sleep patterns in all people, regardless of gender. Animals exhibit different behaviors at different times during the lunar cycle, especially related to hunting and mating. Plants have been shown to move sap through their systems at different rates, depending on whether the moon is waxing or waning.

Our ancestors would have noted these effects on the world around them, planning their hunting, fishing, and foraging activities accordingly. This co-creation with the moon also extended to farming, as the lunar phases governed the best times for planting and harvesting crops during the growing season. In its more visible phases, the moon also provided precious light at night in a world without electricity. It could be argued that the moon's importance to the survival of our ancestors was ultimately just as significant as that of the sun.

Given the crucial roles played by these two celestial bodies, it's no surprise that traditions of sun and moon worship are as old as humanity itself. Together with the Earth, they are part of the structure of the natural world, helping to organize what might otherwise be chaos into form. For witches today, solar and lunar cycles continue to hold spiritual and magical significance.

The Wheel of the Year tradition, found in Wicca and other forms of witchcraft, is rooted in these patterns, with each sabbat celebrating a different point along the annual journey of the sun. Esbats, or lunar sabbats, mark the lunar cycles of the year, typically at each full moon. Green witches may or may not incorporate the Wheel into their practice, but will still observe and work with the turning of the seasons and the rhythms of the moon.

Both the sun and the moon have particularly potent energies to draw on in magic. Many witches like to use both sunlight and moonlight to cleanse and charge crystals, herbs, and other magical allies. Many also use the different energies of the solar and lunar cycles to their advantage in magical work.

Some spells are intended to be worked in daylight, for example, while others are suitable for nighttime. The same is true of spells intended for specific phases in the lunar cycle, as the moon has a different quality of energy when it's full than when it's new. Witches know that by working with the rhythms of light and dark, and waxing and waning, we can align our magic more successfully with the energetic currents of the universe.

THE PLANETS AND THE ZODIAC

Many, but not all, green witches also work with cosmic energies through the observance of astrology, which interprets the positions and movements of the sun, moon, and planets of our solar system in relation to each other, relative to our perspective on Earth.

Before the scientific revolution, astronomy and astrology were the same discipline. The ancients tracked the movement of the sun, moon, and planets across the sky and developed the Zodiac wheel as a measuring system. The 12 divisions within the wheel mark segments of the sky, and each segment, or sign, contains particular energies which influence the planets as they move through them.

The planets themselves also have unique energies, including the sun and moon (which are considered "planets" for the purposes of astrology). All of these diverse energies are constantly interacting with each other in complex ways, with varying degrees of influence on our home planet and its inhabitants.

Astrology has made it possible to predict a variety of phenomena on Earth, from cataclysmic weather events and wars to personality traits, personal life events, and even aspects of physical appearance, according to the positions of the celestial bodies at any given moment in time. However, astrology is still an interpretive art, rather than a "science" by modern definition.

This is in part because of the complexity of the cosmic dance, which includes celestial bodies that were not yet discovered when astrology first emerged. Neptune and Pluto, for example, were not incorporated into interpretations until after their discovery in 1846 and 1930, respectively.

Another reason is that humans have free will, and their astrological makeup can't prevent them from thinking and behaving independently, or evolving as souls during their lifetimes. Human beings are more complex than any single measurement tool can predict. In this sense, astrology is actually more of a language than a science—it describes the energetic underpinnings of people and events.

Astrology is not an inherent focus of green witchcraft per se, but if it interests you, it's worth learning more about as you grow in your practice. Many witches who study astrology find that they understand themselves and others better, and can use their knowledge to make better decisions, time their magical work more skillfully, and make more sense of the world in general.

SHADOW WORK, DIVINE INTELLIGENCE, AND MAGICAL GOALS

Nature's divine intelligence is a useful concept to meditate on when you want to get clear about your magical goals, especially if you've been unsuccessful in spellwork. Exploring your feelings about a situation you want to change can help you choose the best type of spell or magical approach for your particular purposes. This kind of exploration is known in many forms of witchcraft as shadow work, a term coined by analytical psychologist Carl Jung. Shadow work helps us explore the hidden aspects of ourselves that we're not consciously aware of.

So many of the workings of nature happen at a level we can't observe with our five senses. We don't see the sun when it's on the other side of the planet, but it's still there, nurturing life on Earth. We can't see the process of a seed opening, but it's happening under the surface of the soil.

As humans, we also have hidden workings—on the biological level as well as in the very complex realm of emotions, thought patterns, and habits of behavior. Much of who we really are is unknown to us in our conscious minds as we navigate day-to-day life. It's important to take time to slow down, listen to the sounds of our own hearts, and observe our thoughts without judging them.

One way to explore shadow work is through freewriting. Get out some blank writing paper (or your journal, if you already keep one). Then read the following words and spend 10 to 15 minutes writing out whatever comes to mind, using your own magical goal as your focus.

THE WISDOM OF THE FOREST

The forest is a beautiful illustration of the interconnectedness of nature, the forces of light and shadow, and the hidden potential of the unseen.

The tallest trees in a forest absorb the most sunlight. Their canopies of leaves and branches block much of the light from the forest floor, leaving smaller trees and bushes unable to reach the same heights as the great old giants. Yet many of the smaller species need the shade of their taller neighbors in order to survive and thrive.

Every tree, shrub, and plant plays its part in the forest ecosystem, exchanging nutrients and providing food and shelter for birds, insects, and other forest animals. In the diversity of interconnected life within the forest, we can see how nature co-creates with itself, for the benefit of all.

Yet, like the forces at play in any magical working, there's always so much more activity than we can see from our limited perspectives. Birds camouflage their nests in the safety of leafy branches, while mice and salamanders dwell within the hollowed-out logs of fallen trees. Snakes slither under the cover of brown leaves along the forest floor, and here and there a bat blends into a patch of tree bark, sleeping silently until nightfall.

As you consider an aspect of your life that you want to change, ask for divine intelligence to illuminate any hidden aspects yourself that may be blocking manifestation. What have your beliefs about the subject been up until this point? How do you feel, both physically and emotionally, when you think about this issue?

For example, if you earnestly desire a romantic partner but no one is showing up, you might meditate on what aspects of yourself you are allowing to grow and expand. Are you reaching for the sun and allowing yourself to bask in the light? Or are you sheltering somewhat comfortably in the shadow of old beliefs, perhaps about not being "good enough" for a loving relationship?

Is it possible that there are old, stale energies left over from past partners that need to be uprooted and cleared? Maybe there are unhealed emotional or spiritual wounds so entrenched within the soil of your heart that you've forgotten they're there. What underlying issues might you not be seeing that are interconnected with your desire for a relationship?

Whatever your intuition leads you to observe, you can now start to formulate a practical magical intention that will lead you toward your goal. It could be for healing past hurts so that you're ready to move on, or the courage and confidence to put yourself out on the dating scene. Or you may gain insight on the qualities you're looking for in a partner, so that you can include them in the wording of your intention, rather than simply requesting "a lover."

Freewriting and shadow work can be used to help you move forward in any direction you want to go. Whether it's love, money, health, family—any big goal that really means a lot to you will benefit from this kind of inspired examination.

CHAPTER THREE
ELEMENTAL MAGIC

THE CORE ENERGIES OF NATURE

For thousands of years, cultures around the world have recognized that everything in existence arises from one or more fundamental natural phenomena, known today as the *elements*. This knowledge can be traced back to ancient Egypt, Babylonia, and Greece, but is also found in Hinduism, Buddhism, and religions within China and Japan. The elements are also recognized in Australian, Native American, and African traditional spiritual systems.

The number and names of the elements varies across cultures and traditions. Green witches are typically most familiar with the classical Greek elements of earth, air, fire, and water. Chinese cosmology, on the other hand, recognizes fire, water, and earth, but not air, and also includes wood and metal—both key substances for human civilization—which would fall under "earth" in Western traditions. Ancient Tibetan philosophy mirrors the classical Greek system, but includes "space" as a fifth element. The Dagura people of West Africa recognize the five elements of fire, water, earth, mineral, and nature.

The elements are also defined differently from one culture to another. The Greeks believed that the elements were the basic building blocks of life—that all matter was composed of one or more of them, and nothing physical existed outside of them. The Chinese tradition views the elements less as different fixed substances, and more as different forms of energy which is always in flux. Some ancient Indian traditions define the elements as qualities, rather than physical phenomena. For example, water is the quality of being fluid, air is the quality of motion, and fire is the quality of heat.

The elements display the interrelationships inherent to nature in the way they combine and interact to result in the complexity of the natural world. Fire needs earth and air to exist, even as it can consume both. And yet, air can extinguish fire, depending on the amount and force of each, as can earth. Water is both absorbed by earth and able to shape and cover it. Water and air share the ingredient of oxygen, and each can contain the other.

Humans (and all other animals) are also inextricably entwined with the elements. Our bodies make use of earth for fuel, water for substance and sustenance (both in its pure elemental form and in the blood running through our veins), fire for the digestive and reproductive processes, and air for the breath that keeps everything moving. Many traditional healing systems, such as Aryuveda and Chinese medicine, utilize the elements for healing the body, typically by identifying and remedying imbalances within the individual's elemental makeup.

In addition to the classical Greek elements, many, witchcraft traditions also recognize "spirit" as a fifth element. Spirit is what underlies the energy emitted by a crystal, the interaction of a plant with everything visible and invisible in its environment, and the response of water, at the molecular level, to the energies of particular emotions.

It can be thought of as the force behind all of nature's machinations, as well as the life force in every living being (plant, animal, etc.) as well as all elements combined. Spirit infuses us as living beings, both when we are consciously aware of it and when we are not. When we are aware of spirit, and when we have clear, positive intentions, we can utilize this basic core energy to manifest desired change in the world.

Since green witches typically work with the elements of earth, air, fire, and water found throughout the Western Mystery Tradition, these four will be the focus in this guide. However, you may also incorporate spirit as a fifth element in your own practice, or you may even have a different structure altogether. If this is the case, know that you don't have to follow the Western-oriented concept. Go with your own unique perception of the elements.

THE ELEMENTS AND GREEN MAGIC

You may already be aware that each element has particular magical correspondences, or aspects of life that are influenced by its specific energy. In many witchcraft traditions, the elements are linked with the seasons, cardinal directions, zodiac signs, herbs, trees, animals, crystals, and even colors. Green witches may work actively with any, all, or none of these correspondences in their magical practice, but in one way or another they will recognize and connect with elemental energies.

Magical correspondences such as seasons or zodiac signs can help us feel into the energy of the elements in a broadly intuitive way, but the green witch will also benefit from observing how the elements manifest physically in nature. Each element has its own diverse spectrum of energetic potency, emotional mood or tone, and even desirability, from a human perspective. Becoming aware of the range of these qualities within an element, including its less favorable aspects, helps us tune in more to the element's signature energy.

For example:

- **Earth:** think mud, clay, hard-packed dirt in parched deserts, salt flats, cave systems, crystals, boulders, mountains, landslides, rich soil, sand.

- **Air:** think light summer breezes, bitter winter winds, howling hurricanes, stifling humidity, cool dank caves, thunder, leaves fluttering on trees.

- **Fire:** think candle flames, bonfires, lightning, forest blazes, searing hot afternoons, quiet dawns, brilliant sunsets, the brief slices of sunlight on dark winter days.

- **Water:** think creeks, rushing rivers, waterfalls, ocean waves, tranquil lakes, shadowy swamps, underground streams, light sprinkling rains, torrential downpours.

Each form of each element in the natural world shows us an aspect of the element's power, from gentle and harmonious to intense and even dangerous. We don't control this raw power any more than we can control the weather, but we can align with the elements' energies to aid our magical work.

Many witches have a practice of "invoking" the elements, whether as part of a formal ritual (such as in Wicca), or as a means of strengthening their magical work. Consciously inviting the energy of the elements to be present with you, and to merge with the intention you send into the universe, is a powerful act of connecting with nature's intelligence. There's no standard "green witch invocation" ritual to follow, but you can find plenty of ideas from other sources you trust (one is offered in the spell at the end of this chapter), or invent your own. You can also simply speak informally to the elements in your own words.

Keeping an altar with representations of the elements on it is also common among green witches. Those whose practice overlaps with other forms of witchcraft may also include other ritual items, such as deity representations or the traditional tools of Wiccan-style ritual, but these are influences borrowed from ceremonial magic or indigenous religions. They are not inherently "green" traditions. Elemental representations are usually items from nature, such as:

Earth: bowl of soil or sand, crystals and stones, animal bones, acorns
Air: feathers, flowers, natural incense, autumn leaves
Fire: candle, wand of wood or metal, red or orange crystals, sun-dried herbs
Water: bowl of water (dew, rain, spring or tap water), sea shells, blue crystals

Green witches often place the element representations according to their traditional cardinal directions (although you may prefer to come up with your own arrangement):

Earth: North
Air: East
Fire: South
Water: West

Of course, you don't have to keep an altar as a green witch. That's entirely up to you and how you intuit the flow of your own practice. But it is nice to have symbolic representations of the elements somewhere in your daily environment, to help keep the energy of the elements in your living space balanced.

ELEMENTAL QUALITIES AND MAGICAL GOALS

Whether we define the elements as physical manifestations, forms of energy, or some other concept, witches recognize that each element has qualities that relate to an aspect of human experience. For example, matters of financial security are related to earth, while emotions are the domain of water. Air is the realm of ideas and imagination, and fire is the element of transformation.

These qualities can be matched with specific goals or results that we wish to manifest through magical work. A spell for a new job or the means to buy a house would call on earth energy, for instance, while a ritual for healing from a breakup would involve water. Basic elemental correspondences for qualities and magical purposes are detailed in the table at the end of this chapter.

When calling on the energy of a specific element in magical work, you can take the extra step of visualizing an appropriate form of the element as it manifests in nature. Consider your goal in the context of the element—which of its forms is the best match in terms of strength, mood, or energetic style?

For example, if you're working with earth energy for a fertility spell, would you want to visualize a field of rich black soil or a dry, dusty desert? Both represent earth energies, but one is obviously more conducive than the other to birthing new life. If your spell is for cooling off emotional tensions with another person, do you want a nice dip in the lake or a blizzard? Thinking about the elements in this way can help you attune with the *feeling* of what it is you want to accomplish. It is a more vividly focused approach than simply naming the element you're seeking assistance from.

Here are a few more ways to think about linking magical goals with natural imagery in your mind, in order to clarify your focus and amplify the working:

Earth

prosperity: crystals, salt flats
abundance: mountains, sand
grounding: caves, mud, clay

Air

inspiration/new ideas: thunder, fluttering leaves
clear-mindedness (such as for taking a test): fresh air, a brisk wind
success in a difficult conversation: light breeze

Fire

love: candle flames, summer sunshine
courage: lightning, forest fire
resolving anger: sunset

Water

psychic abilities: underground streams
purification: refreshing rain
creative flow: rivers, ocean waves

However you choose to visualize the elements you work with, the most important factor in spellwork is keeping a clear and focused mind. Meditating on a specific elemental image is a useful way to achieve this—simply choose an image to visualize (such as a waterfall, a canyon, a crackling fire, a tree bending in the wind, etc.) and focus on it until it becomes solid and vivid in your mind. Then begin your work.

THE ELEMENTS AND SPIRITUAL ALCHEMY

The elements are powerful allies in spellwork, but their powers go beyond magic in the external world. They also support internal spiritual alchemy, helping us identify and play to our personal strengths, and illuminating aspects of ourselves—various personality traits, attitudes, habits, and thought patterns—that block manifestations from coming through on the physical plane. This kind of introspection is another form of shadow work, which we discussed in Chapter 2. Learning about the personal qualities associated with each element can help you identify where some inner transformation would benefit you.

Humans are born with one or two predominant elements that characterize their personality, or their way of perceiving and interacting with the world. Predominant elements often correspond with our personal strengths, but they present challenges when they're out of balance. When we tune into elemental energy to navigate our own human nature, we can transform our inner lives, which always results in positive changes in our outer lives.

One way to identify your elemental makeup is through your astrological birth chart. In Western astrology, your sun sign is considered to be your main element, but you may also have several planets in a different element, so it's useful to have this information. Zodiac associations are also listed in the table at the end of this chapter.

However, it's not entirely necessary to know your personal astrology to do this work. As you read the descriptions below, you may find yourself resonating with one or two elements more than the others. If so, this is likely your area of most successful alchemy.

Earth

Alchemy keywords: patience, permanence, diligence, commitment, discipline

Earth people are practically-minded, reliable, and disciplined, with an innate sense for the workings of the material world. Their methodical approach to work often enables them to achieve material security with greater ease than other elemental personalities.

However, even the most sensible habits and patterns of living can become overly rigid. It can be difficult for those with Earth as their dominant energy to feel comfortable in the face of dynamic change. They may not always realize that security is, like everything else, ultimately impermanent, that growth is cyclical, and that there are always unseen forces which we may not be able to control, but can make an effort to better understand. Without a certain amount of flexibility and trust, we can't be open to higher-frequency energies that inspire us with new perspectives and motivate us to set our sights on new horizons.

Air

Alchemy keywords: inspiration, imagination, knowledge, objectivity

Air people tend to have very active minds and feel at home in the realms of abstract thought. They have a knack for discovering new ideas, and a higher degree of emotional detachment and objectivity than those with other dominant elements. They are socially energetic and take an interest in the ideas of others, but their dynamic nature and need for movement and free expression may keep them from hanging around in one place for any length of time.

Air people need to learn to appreciate the value in being still, as well as being in touch with their emotions, which can often be an uncomfortable realm for them. They would do well to balance their flightiest, high-level energies with more grounded, fixed energies, or else all of that intellectual potential may stay unmanifested in the material world.

Fire

Alchemy keywords: strength, willpower, initiative, enthusiasm

Fire people are generally enthusiastic, vigorous, impassioned, and easily excitable. Courageous and willing to charge forth, they are natural leaders, and they often feel passionate enough about causes or goals that nothing gets in the way of their drive to succeed.

However, they can also be impulsive and somewhat insensitive compared to other elemental personalities. They may struggle with a perceived need for immediate gratification or have the tendency to be in a hurry all the time. Too much fire energy can make a person quick-tempered or even prone to rage. Fire people can benefit from learning to ease up on the fuel when appropriate, and taking a more long-range view of what will be needed to sustain that energy beyond the present moment. Slowing down and cooling off does not have to mean being extinguished, but can instead be a wise way to ensure success in the long run.

Water

Alchemy keywords: reflection, psychic ability, love, generosity, empathy

The most naturally intuitive of all the elemental personalities, water people can be incredibly sensitive to the moods and energies of others. They tend to have a deep understanding of the makeup and motives of the human psyche, and make for good listeners and healers. They are often creative types, with mystical leanings and an appreciation for the sensual. They tend to be more at home in their emotions than those with other dominant elements.

However, too much water can lead to intense emotionality and difficulty maintaining psychic boundaries. Water people can be overly sensitive, to the point that they are essentially immobilized by all of the stimuli around them and risk drowning in other people's emotions and energies. They can also succumb to laziness and lethargy if their energy frequencies are too low. Water people will benefit from physical movement and grounding activities to balance their energy.

ELEMENTAL BALANCE SPELL

This working initiates the process of balancing an overly dominant element in your life. This may be your predominant element, or just an element that corresponds to something you're struggling with.

You will use your creativity to design a personalized alchemical ritual based on your specific situation. You may wish to draw from the spiritual alchemy descriptions above for inspiration.

Note: You will be releasing the elemental representations back into nature, so choose items you don't wish to keep.

Spell items:

- Elemental representations (1 from each element, see the altar discussion above for suggestions)
- Work candle for atmosphere
- Journal or writing paper

Instructions:

Light the work candle and take three deep breaths. When you feel ready, call upon the elements to lend their energies to your spell, using the following (or similar) words:

"With reverence for the divine intelligence of nature, I call upon the elements of earth, air, fire, and water to be with me at this time."

Now spend some time writing about the issue you're seeking assistance with, and identify the element that needs balancing. For example, if you're struggling to accept or adapt to a major change in your life, the element at play may be earth.

Keeping the interrelationships of the elements in mind, feel into which one naturally suggests itself as a balance for the issue. Earth can be moved by wind or water, dried out by the sun, or cracked open by movements in the earth's fiery core. Which element embodies the qualities you need most at this time? (You may wish to review the alchemy keywords for each element, above, for help with this.)

Arrange the elemental representations in a circle on your altar or work space, using their traditional cardinal directions, or whichever placements feel right to you. Now pick up the representation of the element that needs balancing, and say the following (or similar) words:

"The element of [name element] is too much with me at this time. I am choosing to release what isn't serving me."

Set the representation in the center of the circle, and pick up the representation of the element you're using to restore the balance.

Visualize a form of this element in nature that best fits your sense of what is needed (for example, a rain that softens the soil, or a more forceful rain that carries it away). Hold this vision in your mind as you say the following (or similar) words:

"I now call forth the element of [name element] to balance the [name element] within."

Sit quietly for a few moments with your eyes closed, and notice how your body feels. When the work feels complete, open your eyes and thank the elements for their assistance with this spell.

Gather the elemental representations and return them to nature, beginning with the element you needed to balance, and ending with the element you chose for assistance.

ELEMENTAL CORRESPONDENCES

The qualities and magical purposes listed here are commonly recognized in many, but not necessarily all, forms of witchcraft. You may come across differences if you look to several different sources. (The zodiac associations, on the other hand, are universal.)

These lists are by no means exhaustive, and you may perceive elemental qualities differently. Always work with what feels most authentic to you.

Element	Primary Qualities	Magical Purposes	Zodiac Signs	Season
Earth	Grounding, stability, endurance, discipline, prosperity, abundance	Fertility, luck, longevity, success in endeavors, employment, business, money	Capricorn, Taurus, Virgo	Winter
Air	Intellect, ideas, imagination, communication, expression	Concentration, clarity, inspiration, knowledge, wisdom, harmony	Aquarius, Gemini, Libra	Spring
Fire	Passion, enthusiasm, illumination, transformation, *creativity (*action/ignition)	Joy, love, strength, motivation, willpower, courage, resolving anger	Aries, Leo, Sagittarius	Summer
Water	Emotion, sensitivity, intuition, empathy, generosity, love, *creativity (*flow of inspiration)	Healing, purification, friendship, love, relationship issues, psychic abilities	Pisces, Cancer, Scorpio	Autumn

CHAPTER FOUR
SEASONAL AND LUNAR MAGIC

LIFE, DEATH, AND REBIRTH

Green witchcraft is ultimately a practice of working in rhythm with the natural world. The changing seasons offer us ongoing opportunities to connect and work with nature's divine intelligence, as seasons are themselves natural manifestations of divine energy.

Each season has its own moods, qualities, and magical associations that can help us engage with aspects of ourselves on a deeper level, recognize the blessings in our lives, and clarify our desires, goals, and intentions for the future. When we tune in to the natural rhythms of the planet, allowing ourselves to be guided by the spiritual energies available at different times of the year, we experience life and all of its magic in a more dynamic and fulfilling way.

That said, not all seasons are equally magical to everyone. Many people prefer the warm temperatures and lush growth of summer, while others thrive in colder seasons and don't mind the bleakness of winter. And while it's common for people to struggle with the diminishing daylight that begins in autumn, the spring's shift back into longer days is actually more difficult for others to acclimate to. Every season brings challenges as well as blessings.

Yet we can learn to appreciate even our least favorite time of year when we approach it from an appreciation of divine intelligence. Green witches learn to honor the roles of both creation and destruction in the cycles of nature—the green growth of spring and summer and the death and barrenness of fall and winter. We recognize that each has its part to play in the ongoing creation of life on planet Earth, all of which is governed by life/death/rebirth cycles. All living things take part in the processes of fertilization, emergence, growth, maturity, death, and decomposition. We can witness these processes up close in the life cycles of plants. In fact, you could even say that plants themselves have their own seasons.

Although there is obviously a lot of variation between different kinds of plants (flowers, shrubs, trees, herbs, wild vs. cultivated plant life, etc.), a basic pattern is seen throughout the plant kingdom. With a few exceptions (like mosses and ferns), every plant begins as a seed. Given the right conditions of soil, water and light, the seed will root and send up shoots above the soil. As the seedling reaches upward toward the sun, leaves begin to develop, followed by buds which become flowers. The flowers are pollinated by bees, wasps, moths, butterflies, bats, or wind, and this produces the fruit of the plant. The fruit (or nut, or cone) contains the seeds that will start the next cycle of growth.

Once the fruit has reached its ripest point, it will drop to the ground, or in the case of flowers, its seeds will be scattered by the wind. The fruit may also be eaten by insects, birds, or other animals. Either way, the seeds within will ultimately find their way back into the soil, beginning the cycle all over again. The plant itself will eventually die, but its remains will still support many different life forms, from invisible microorganisms (which help create new soil) to earthworms and insects, and, in the case of trees, larger animals that make their homes in dead trunks and branches. The dead plant also "lives on" in whatever new plants grow in the soil into which it decomposed, which has been enriched by the plant's decaying nutrients.

This eternal ebb and flow is most easily observed in annual plants, which complete their life cycle in one growing season. Trees take much longer to live out their full cycle, but they enact the processes of shedding and regeneration throughout their lives, as we can see with leaf cycles of deciduous trees, and the fruits and cones of evergreens. But the energies of the life/death/rebirth cycle are also reflected in the changes of the shifting seasons, as well as the phases of the moon, which we will see a bit later in this chapter.

SEASONAL ENERGIES

Depending on where you live, the changes in weather and daylight patterns from season to season may be subtle or very pronounced. Seasonal differences tend to be most dramatic in the temperate zones of the Northern Hemisphere, but all regions experience some amount of shifting between one season and another. The discussion below is oriented to the seasonal patterns of the Northern Hemisphere, as this is where much of contemporary witchcraft has its roots.

Since ancient times, people have observed the solstices and the equinoxes as important markers in the sun's journey (viewed from our perspective) around the Earth. Our modern calendars designate the beginning and end of each season according to these solar markers. However, in terms of how the seasons manifest in nature, the cross-quarter days (or the halfway mark between each solar point) are usually where the shift from one to the next is more evident.

For example, spring is said to begin on or around March 20, depending on where the exact moment of the spring equinox falls on the Gregorian calendar. But early February is typically when the icy grip of winter begins to loosen and the first signs of spring emerge. Summer doesn't officially end until mid-September, but by early August the waning daylight is evident, and the growing season begins to wind down. Many ancient cultures held these cross-quarter days to be equally spiritually important as the solstices and equinoxes, if not more so.

The Celts recognized the beginning of May (Beltane) as the start of summer, and early November (Samhain) as the start of winter. These cross-quarter dates came to be "fixed" with the adoption of the modern calendar as February 2, May 1, August 1, and October 31, but in reality, these occasions were determined either by the astronomical halfway point between the two adjoining solar markers, or by signals from nature. For example, Beltane was not celebrated until the first blossoms appeared on the hawthorn trees.

Green witches may or may not celebrate the eight points along the Wheel of the Year, as is done in many witchcraft traditions. But we do honor the changing of the seasons in our own individual ways, and work with the energies that each season brings. Below is an overview of the flow of nature's energies throughout the year, but it is by no means comprehensive or universally recognized by all green witches. While magical associations are detailed here, this doesn't imply working for a particular magical purpose is limited to the designated season. It's just that these are especially compatible energies for the work at this time.

WINTER

Winter is the season of stillness and quietude. The earth is resting from the previous year's growing season, in order to be ready for the next one to begin. Both above and below ground, many forms of life are in hibernation. The cold temperatures keep humans indoors more than out, making this a season of introspection and grounding. The long nights and bitter weather can seem endless at times, but this is an invitation from nature to get plenty of rest, and to cultivate patience with things that are outside of our control.

Winter is also about material security and a focus on the hearth and home, as this time of year was potentially deadly for anyone who didn't have enough food and fuel to last them into spring. This is the season of the earth element, making it ideal for magic relating to all aspects of financial and personal well-being.

The cross-quarter day between the winter solstice and the spring equinox marks the "quickening," the first stirrings of new life beneath the still-cold ground. The warmer temperatures after the long period of cold spurs seeds to open and prepare to sprout. As winter finally begins to thaw, we turn our attention back toward the outer world and begin to plan for the new manifestations we want to create.

Magical Associations: money, employment, real estate, resolving debt and paying bills, physical healing, safety and security, patience, endurance

SPRING

Spring makes itself known through the sudden appearance of buds and blossoms on the trees. This is the season of fertility and renewal, as green shoots emerge from the ground and "spring fever" takes hold of the animals (and humans, too!) The energy is much more active now, and witches who keep gardens will be preparing beds and planting seeds. There is also an aspect of purification to this energy, of opening the closed-up spaces that sheltered us through the winter and allowing new, fresh air to move freely through.

Spring is the season of the air element, bringing us inspiration, curiosity, and new ideas. We are encouraged to slough off old ways of thinking and imagine new manifestations to channel our renewed energy into. Magic related to growth, whether spiritual, intellectual, or material, is favored at this time.

In just a few short weeks, the new leaves on the trees will have transformed the landscape. Seeds planted at the start of the season will have become seedlings which will grow stronger as the daylight continues to increase. This is a wonderful moment to appreciate the beauty all around you, before the sultry heat of summer arrives.

Magical Associations: purification, fertility, growth, gardening, inspiration, wisdom

SUMMER

Summer is the season of beauty, abundance, and vitality. The growing season is now in full swing, and the long days ensure plenty of opportunity to enjoy time outdoors. This is the season of the fire element, as the sun is at its strongest, bringing with it the energies of passion and creativity. It's a good time for magic relating to relationships of all kinds, physical energy and well-being, and anything else that brings you joy.

There is also an aspect of potential impatience or even anger, as seen when people get grouchy during a heat wave. The invitation here is to stay aware of "hot" emotions and cultivate positive vibrations by appreciating beauty. The vision of a soon-to-unfold flower is a powerful metaphor for the delicious anticipation of new creations coming forth, and a good lesson in the importance of trusting divine timing—you cannot hurry the flower's process.

Traditionally, the first harvest begins midway through the summer at the cross-quarter day, as we slowly shift away from the height of the sun's power. But there are still some warm, bright days ahead before autumn arrives in earnest.

Magical Associations: friendship, love, marriage, strength, physical stamina, courage, protection, abundance (in all forms)

AUTUMN

Autumn brings with it the full shift from growing season to harvest, as the days become noticeably shorter than just weeks ago. This season highlights the importance of gratitude, for the bounty of the fields, for the fruits of our own efforts over the past two seasons, and for anything and everything that we appreciate in our lives. Of course, this is always a good practice to be in, especially if you want to manifest more of what you want—the higher your vibrational frequency, the better results you will get. But this is a particularly good time for gratitude, as we prepare to enter the dark time of the year.

As the season of the water element, Autumn is also about reflection, intuition, and examining our inner landscape. Magic related to emotional issues and psychic receptivity is particularly potent during this time. It's also a good time for letting go of unhealthy habits (both physical and mental) and deepening your study of magic.

By the cross-quarter point, the leaves have turned and the trees get barer with each passing day, and the ground is more brown than green. We, too, are invited to release what no longer serves us in order to make room for the new manifestations to be born. Traditionally, autumn is the season of death, but from nature's point of view, there is no true death. Everything that dies is recycled into nature's overall system, including humans, whose souls will reincarnate into new bodies in new lifetimes. We take comfort in remembering this as we head into the stillness of winter.

Magical Associations: reaping benefits from past efforts, emotional healing, releasing bad habits, banishing, psychic ability

LUNAR SEASONS

The life/death/rebirth cycle is honored in many witchcraft traditions by observing the rhythmic shifts of the moon. Over the course of each 28-day cycle, the moon appears to be born, grow, recede, and "die" before being reborn again. These lunar phases are also a bit like seasons, with different energies shifting through each part of the cycle. The shifts are much more subtle than those of the seasons, and are typically undetected altogether by most people (with the possible exception of the full moon, when lunar energy is at its strongest). But when we practice paying attention to each phase of the cycle, we can tune into these different energies, and we can even tailor our magical work accordingly

The lunar calendar divides the moon's cycle into four even quarters, but from a magical standpoint, the appearance of the moon as it moves through the cycle is more relevant to working with its energies. The new moon isn't actually visible until a few days in, when it emerges as a thin crescent shape. The crescent then fills out to a half-circle by the middle of the waxing phase, growing into its near-full circle (or "gibbous") shape in the days leading up to the full moon. Then the process reverses, as the full moon appears to shrink gradually back to gibbous, then half, then fades back into a waning crescent before it disappears altogether.

Witches work their craft in tandem with these expanding and contracting energies. When the moon is growing larger (waxing), we work magic for increase, or attracting desired circumstances into our lives. When the moon is fading away (waning), we work for elimination of unwanted circumstances from our lives. As the midpoint of the cycle, the full moon is a time to celebrate the blessings in our lives and begin to identify what we want to release once the waning phase begins. When the new moon returns, with its promise of new things to come, it's time to set our intentions for increase again.

The shifts in lunar energy as it moves through each phase align with both seasonal energies and the stages of the life/death/rebirth cycle (see the table on the following page).

Witches also recognize a final phase of the cycle called the "dark moon." This is the brief period after the waning crescent disappears and before the new moon begins. Because the moon seems to have faded into death, this phase doesn't have a life cycle alignment, but in terms of seasonal energy it can be thought of as the "dead" of winter.

The energy can feel flat, disorienting, or even unsettling during this period. There is a sense of time standing still. Many witches see the dark moon as a time for rest, and refrain from active magical work. Some might use this energy to communicate with ancestors or loved ones in the spirit world, or engage in shadow work, as the dark moon is an ideal time for inner reflection.

Moon Phase	Life Cycle Phase	Solar Seasonal Marker	Season	Magical Focus
New	Seed	Cross-quarter day (Feb 2)	Late Winter / Early Spring	Setting intentions, initiating new projects
Waxing Crescent	Root	Spring Equinox	Spring	Attracting/increase
Waxing Half	Leaf	Cross-quarter day (May 1)	Late Spring / Early Summer	Attracting/increase
Half to Full (Gibbous)	Bud	Summer Solstice	Summer	Attracting/increase
Full	Flower	Cross-quarter day (Aug 1)	Late Summer / Early Autumn	Celebration of abundance and blessings
Full to Half (Gibbous)	Fruit	Autumn Equinox	Autumn	Releasing/decrease
Waning Half	Harvest	Cross-quarter day (Oct 31)	Late Autumn / Early Winter	Releasing/decrease
Waning Crescent	Compost	Winter Solstice	Winter	Releasing/banishing, divination, shadow work

THE MAGIC OF CHANGE

Taken as a whole, the deeper magic of the moon and of the seasons is in what they teach us about change, which is the only constant in life, and which is also what magic *always is*. When we work for a magical goal, we are working to create change. Even if the work is about protection, the intention is for the outcome to be different from whatever it is we're protecting against.

Humans naturally like consistency and tend to struggle with change, even when we know it's ultimately to our benefit. Like seasonal shifts, change can be sudden or gradual, smooth or chaotic, expected or unexpected, welcome or unwelcome. But viewed in the right light, change is always a catalyst for new experiences and spiritual growth.

Working with the energies of the seasons and lunar phases is an empowered way to make the most of our magic and to navigate the more uncomfortable aspects of change. Surrendering to these cycles is a way of letting go—we can't control how our magical manifestations unfold in our lives any more than we can control the seasons or the moon's appearance in the sky.

But when we hold the intention for what we desire while releasing the need to know exactly how or when it will manifest, we are flowing with the changing energetic rhythms of the universe. This leads to more enjoyment of each day, no matter the position of the sun or moon.

Here are some simple yet powerful magical workings to help you integrate seasonal energies into your life. These can be done in their designated season or their corresponding moon phase. (For best results, use both if you can!)

WINTER DREAM SPELL

Moon phase: waning crescent into new moon

As the season of rest, and a time when the energies around us feel somewhat subterranean, winter is perfect for dream magic. As you prepare to go to bed, brew a tea of chamomile, mugwort, passionflower, and/or peppermint. Light a candle, and as you sip your tea, do some journaling about any issue you'd like to get clarity about at this time. If you could have one question answered about this issue right now, what would it be? Write the question down. When you're finished journaling, gently extinguish the candle.

When you go to bed, leave your journal (or other writing paper) and pen close by. Before you fall asleep, restate your question and set an intention to receive an answer in your dreams. (You may get an answer in one dream, or in several parts across several dreams.) As soon as you wake up, write down everything you can remember about what you dreamed in the night. If none of it seems relevant to your question, leave it be for now and re-read your dream notes at a later time. Sometimes it takes awhile for the subconscious symbolism to emerge into clarity.

SPRING SEED INTENTION SPELL

Moon phase: new moon through waxing moon

A seed is a very small packet of big, highly charged energy. All the potential of a new manifestation is contained within this seemingly insignificant speck of matter. Whether a given seed becomes a flower or a tree depends on the specific information stored within it. Whether it opens, develops, and flourishes depends on various environmental factors, but flourish is what it's designed to do.

Our magical intentions are like seeds. We "plant" them through spellwork, and then wait as patiently as we can for them to manifest into our reality. But we often hinder their progress by checking on them before they're ready, or giving up before they have the chance to materialize.

Choose an intention you'd like to manifest over the coming six months. Write it on a small slip of paper and fold the slip until it's as small as you can get it. Choose a place outside to bury the folded paper in the earth. Pour a bit of water onto the soil where the buried "seed" lies and visualize the paper unfolding, sending up shoots, taking root, and ultimately becoming the outcome you desire.

Now let go and let nature's divine timing do the rest. Any time you feel doubt about your goal, remember the "seed" transforming under the soil, water it with positive energy, and let the universe do its work.

SUMMER FIRE RITUAL

Moon phase: waxing moon into full moon

As the warmest and brightest part of the year, summer's energy is a natural time for amplifying joy and well-being. But it's also well-suited for addressing any fears that hold us back from truly enjoying life. Fire embodies the energy of courage and banishes darkness with its light. This ritual helps you connect with your own inner fire to follow your passions, without being ruled by fear of what could go wrong.

You'll need a large candle, a pair of tongs or long-armed match-holder, a heat-proof dish, a pen, and a small slip of paper. For added energy, gather some fire crystals like carnelian, citrine, tiger's eye, and garnet (or any red, orange, and/or yellow stones).

Place the stones in a circle around the candle. Light the candle and take three deep breaths. Then write down the word "fear" on a small slip of paper (or name a specific fear, if you wish). Using the tongs, ignite the paper and watch as it burns to ash over the heat-proof dish.

Sit for a few moments, visualizing a bright, protective white and gold light infusing your body, and surrounding you and your work space. When you feel the work is complete, gently extinguish the candle, and scatter the ashes over the earth.

AUTUMN CLEARING-OUT RITUAL

Moon phase: full moon through waning moon

Autumn signifies the time when the old must die in order to make room for the new. This is ideal energy for clearing out your closet, wardrobe, junk drawers, or any other part of your home where clutter congregates, causing energy to become stagnant. Let go of things you no longer wear or use, and pass them on to others who will benefit from them. Donate, recycle, or repurpose your items as much as possible to keep them out of landfills.

If you have a hard time deciding what to give away, let your heart be your guide. Hold an item you're unsure about in your hands and take note of how you feel. Items with sentimental value may be worth keeping, but only if they truly bring you joy. Any other emotion is a signal that it's time to release your attachment to whatever the item represents, and getting rid of the item is an excellent place to start.

When you're finished clearing out, notice the change in how you feel in your living space. Smudge with sage or lavender and say a few words of appreciation both for what you've released, and for the new things that will flow into your life.

CHAPTER FIVE
GREEN DIVINATION

NATURE IS TALKING TO YOU

Generally speaking, divination is the practice of interacting with the spiritual plane in order to find information or insight into a situation. This can be done with material tools like crystal balls, tea leaves, Tarot cards, or runes, and green witches might work with any of these or other divination methods. But divination can also happen without any human-made tools.

You can receive messages from nature on a simple walk through the woods, or sitting quietly on a river bank. Trees, flowers, animals, rocks, and even the wind and sky are physical embodiments of the spiritual energy that permeates all things. When you are open to this energy and the subtle nudges it sends you through your intuition, you can tap into the wisdom of the universe.

In fact, much of the ancient knowledge of medicinal plants was obtained through direct receptivity to spiritual energies of nature. The shamans, folk healers, and medicine people of indigenous cultures were able to communicate with the spirits of plants. They learned from the plants themselves which ones were beneficial for humans and which were dangerous or even deadly.

Of course, trial and error were also involved, no doubt with some fatal mistakes now and again (and this is a good reminder to never touch or ingest a plant you're not familiar with!) But without the connection to the spiritual plane, there would have been no way to know where to begin learning the benefits of the plants that grew in the world around them.

In contrast to the Tarot, runes, or the I Ching, "green" divination is not a specific practice with steps to follow, or established interpretations for any signs or symbols that may present themselves. You can try taking a hike with the intention of finding out the answer to a specific question, but nature may not be inclined to conform to your expectations the way a formal divination tool is designed to do. However, when you're dealing with something that you need to get perspective on, being in nature can help you see aspects of the situation—or of yourself—that you've been too clouded by stress or emotion to understand.

Nature talks to us in many different ways. Sometimes we may get a specific message just for us, but often we're simply receiving a general acknowledgment of our presence, and of our value to the overall system of divine intelligence. Nature uses the elements as well as animals and nonphysical spirit beings to communicate with us. The more time you spend in nature with a quiet and open mind, the more you will develop your own personal ways of intuiting the messages the universe is bringing to you.

ELEMENTAL COMMUNICATION

Just as the elements can lend their energies to our magical work, they can also be conduits through which the universe communicates with us. A burst of embers from a crackling bonfire might affirm something you've just spoken, or warn against an idea you've just had. The same can happen with thunder and lightning, or a sudden wave on a calm sea.

Scrying is a divination term for the art of seeing images in a reflective surface. We typically associate scrying with crystal balls or bowls of water, but nature offers countless "surfaces" where images may appear. In addition to glassy lakes, ponds and puddles, you can perceive visual messages in bonfire flames, clouds, trees, and potentially anything else you see.

You can find images in the lines and color variations of seashells and common stones. You might even see significance in the patterns on a shoreline made from incoming waves, or tracks made by animals in the snow. The secret to scrying is to gaze with a soft focus and keep your mind open. Don't actively look for anything. Just see what arises when you relax your visual focus.

Watching the clouds for shapes and faces as they float by is an easy way to practice scrying outdoors. Trees also make excellent mediums for nonphysical energy to communicate through, particularly in the summer months when they are fully fleshed out with leaves. If you soften your gaze when looking at them, you'll likely find that all kinds of faces pop out among the leaves, as well as on trunks and branches.

Wind is a fun and powerful method through which nature can communicate with you. Have you ever watched a tree and noticed just two or three leaves fluttering in a breeze while the rest of the tree is still? It may be a nature spirit letting you know it's there. The next time you're having an introspective moment and a sudden gust of wind blows through, consider what your most recent thought was. You might be getting confirmation of an idea or insight. Windy days can also be particularly good for scrying among leafy trees and fast-moving clouds, as both can create moving pictures.

Speaking of nature spirits, this is another term with different meanings for different people. Because everyone perceives and interacts with nonphysical energy in their own unique way, green witches have diverse concepts of spirit beings in the natural world. Some perceive what they understand to be faeries, while others may call them "earth spirits" or *genii locorum* (spirits of a place). These spirits may inhabit a tree, a flower, or an entire area, such as a grove or a lake. Some witches assign different kinds of nature spirits to each of the four elements, while others view all as part of the element of spirit.

You may not see or hear nature spirits when in their presence—this ability to experience them with physical senses is actually fairly rare. Instead, many describe an awareness of a subtle presence, or a shift in the energy of their surroundings. Visible or not, however, these spirits can still call your attention to things. They may even present themselves as the face in the tree trunk you've been staring at, or a light breeze on your shoulder.

If you're out in the wilderness and come across a place that feels uncomfortable or foreboding, consider the possibility that you're being warned about something. Witches have had poison ivy and other hazards pointed out to them by nature spirits, simply by picking up on a shift in energy and having a good look around before proceeding. That said, nature spirits may or may not care to communicate with you. When it comes to taking care of the environment, humans don't have the best track record, and it may take time to develop a relationship with the spirit(s) of a given place.

One way to begin such a relationship is by bringing offerings. Traditions vary regarding what constitutes an offering, but common items include flowers, small crystals and shiny stones, herbs, honey, a few splashes of wine or milk, small fruits, and small handfuls of grain. Some green witches prefer to bring water, which the soil can always make use of. (Nature spirits do appreciate assistance in improving the quality of their home.) But don't leave cooked food, or anything that might harm local wildlife, and only use natural items. Leave the offering wherever your intuition guides you.

Whether or not nature spirits take interest in you personally, learning to be aware of and attuning to their subtle energies is good practice for communicating with nature as a whole, as it helps you attune to your unique spiritual path.

ANIMAL MESSENGERS

Animals have different means of perception from humans, and many are able to see, hear, and smell things that human senses don't register. Animals can also be easily influenced by unseen energy, and so can be communicators of that energy. It's always worth noting any unusual animal sightings, or even common animal sightings that seem somehow significant. (And if you dream about an animal, it's fairly safe to say there's a message there!)

In indigenous cultures around the world, animals embody many different kinds of wisdom for humans to learn from. Interpretations of animal messages vary across traditions, but are usually rooted in mythological associations and/or aspects of the animal's natural behavior. Spiders, for example, symbolize the virtues of patience and persistence, as well as the importance of viewing a situation from every angle. Deer can point to an upcoming new adventure and let you know that you are being gently encouraged to take advantage of it.

Squirrels are thought to bring a message of the importance of balancing work and play. Depending on your circumstances when squirrels come into your awareness, they may be reminding you to take a break and go have some fun, or signaling that you need to be sure your material bases are covered. The crow, long associated with warnings of death, can also appear to those on the spiritual path on the eve of some kind of personal transformation.

Furthermore, your deceased loved ones in the spirit world can, and often do, come to you in the form of animals. This could be any animal in your vicinity, but it happens quite often with birds, butterflies, and other brightly-colored animals that stay in your presence for just a short time. So, if you've ever "felt" the presence of someone on the other side when a particular animal is around, you can bet that you received a visit!

Sometimes it will be quite obvious that there's a message, such as when a wild animal suddenly enters your house, or appears in some other unusual place. But often it can be more subtle. For example, maybe you've noticed that you keep seeing robins whenever you're worrying about a particular problem in your life. Or perhaps a rabbit shoots suddenly across the grass while you're in deep conversation with a friend. There is a wealth of information in books and online sources you can turn to for interpretations of these animal communications, so look up any animal that catches your attention, and see if any resonate with you.

These moments can be seen as invitations to pause, take a step back, and seek a new perspective on whatever has been going on in your life. They could also be signals to stay open to new developments that are just around the corner. Take a moment to communicate with the spirit energy of any animal that crosses your path in a distinctive way. Thank it for visiting you, and do some research to find out more specifically what it has to say to you. As you make a deliberate practice of acknowledging these visitations, the universe will respond by sending you even more messages from the animal kingdom.

Of course, not every sighting of an animal is necessarily significant—as they say, sometimes a bird is just a bird. (However, if you're dreaming about a bird, it's probably not just a bird.) The same can be said of a sudden wind or a face in the clouds. Be aware of getting too caught up in nature's mysteries and reading everything that happens in every moment as a "sign."

On a related note, don't worry too much about "correctly" interpreting the messages you receive from nature. What you pick up on may be reflecting something about your inner process or present circumstances, but it may also just be about connecting with the divine mystery, and allowing your spirit to engage in some much-needed "play time." When you seek to commune with nature, what you resonate with on a personal level is what you're meant to tune in to.

OPEN YOUR CHANNEL TO NATURE'S WISDOM

You don't have to travel to the wilderness to open your own channel of communication with the divine energy of nature. Natural energy is everywhere, including in your own backyard, your nearest local park, or anywhere that living things grow. So find the nearest place to where you live that you can spend some time attuning to and connecting with the spiritual energies of nature. Bring your journal (if you keep one), and an offering for the spirits of the place.

Come into this exercise without any expectations. If you're looking to see or experience something in particular, you may miss what the spirit of nature is offering you. Start by closing your eyes and take a few deep breaths, in through your nose and out through your mouth.

Then simply begin exploring the area with your physical senses. Get up close and personal with the trees and other plant life. Look closely at leaves, stems, branches, bark, the ground under your feet, the sky above you. Notice any birds or other wildlife (including insects!) and simply watch their behavior. Also note the sounds and scents of the area. Depending on where you are, these may include human or urban noises and smells, but they too are part of the energetic tapestry of this place.

Once you feel fully present to the area, start paying attention to your emotional energy. How does what you *feel* shift as you move to different locations within the space? How do you feel standing near one tree versus another? What about sitting near a specific plant?

These subtle changes are different currents of the natural energies in the area interacting with you. As you explore them, feel into where the best place would be to leave your offering, and do so. Let the spirits of the place know you appreciate them and are open to any communication that benefits you at this time. (You can say this silently if you're in a public place and don't want to draw attention to yourself.)

Now find a place to sit comfortably and write about your experiences in your journal—any thoughts, impressions, or questions that come to mind. You can also just meditate for awhile, if you prefer. When you're ready to leave, thank the spirits of the place for sharing energy with you. Take note again of how you feel. How has this experience changed your energy today?

Note that this practice may or may not bring you a clear answer to any questions on your mind. The objective is to open up and attune to the spiritual energies of nature, which will hone your intuition and psychic receptivity. This, in turn, helps you become a better reader of Tarot or any other divination tools you work with. But establishing a direct connection with nature's divine intelligence is a reward in and of itself, and will serve you in many ways along your path.

CHAPTER SIX
PLANTS AND THE GREEN WITCH

THE MAGICAL PLANT KINGDOM

The world of plants is a core aspect of green witchcraft, and for good reason: they are simply magical. As we have seen, plants represent the most obvious manifestations of the life/death/rebirth cycles in nature. Plants have amazing sensory capacities and communicate with each other, as well as with humans who are able to pick up on their spiritual energies.

Like humans, plants are delicate and vulnerable, yet resilient in times of stress or danger. Plants look out for each other by sharing crucial nutrients and warning each other, through chemical signals, of impending attacks from hungry insects. These intelligent beings are also crucial to life on Earth, as animals (including humans) depend on them for survival.

Beyond survival, however, plants also make it easier for humans to thrive, as they can be incredibly multifunctional. Many herbs are used medicinally as well as in cooking. In the form of essential oils, plants are transformed into aromatherapeutic remedies for a dizzying array of ailments from anxiety to muscle tension to tinnitus, as well as household cleaners and pest deterrents. And of course, plants have incredible magical properties that lend themselves to spellwork of all kinds. Truly, plants are a green witch's best friends!

Take lavender, for example. This fragrant flowering herb has been used ritually, medicinally, and cosmetically since the days of ancient Rome. Lavender has healing properties, particularly for the skin, as well as antiseptic and antibacterial properties. It also reduces anxiety and promotes restful sleep. It's long been a staple ingredient in soaps, skin care products and perfumes, can help repel moths, and can even be used in baking and cooking. Magically, lavender is a powerful love herb, but can also be used for protection, clairvoyance, purification and consecration of sacred space, and emotional healing. All of these benefits contained in just one plant—what a wonderful gift from nature!

There are three main ways to bring plants into your magical practice: harvesting from plants in the wild, growing your own garden, and keeping houseplants (houseplants are discussed in Chapter 7). But before you bring any new green lovelies into your space, always remember to research whether the plant is toxic to people or pets—especially if you have small children or animals who like to munch on leaves.

Another important thing to know is the difference between scientific names and common names for plants. Common names, or folk names, are what we typically use when we talk about plants. A given plant is known by many different names in various cultures, although there is plenty of overlap between cultures. Plants were named for various characteristics, including their physical appearance, their medicinal and/or psychoactive properties, their dangers, and even their use in witchcraft.

For example, mandrake was known in several European languages as "sorcerer's root," "magic root," and "witches' herb," as well as "witches' love herb" and "enchanter's nightshade." These names clearly show that mandrake was used for magical purposes (and likely more than once in a love spell!) But it was also known as "little man" and "human plant," due to its root's resemblance to the human form. Mandrake has narcotic and hallucinogenic effects, which may be why it was called "devil's herb" and "madness herb," but it was also used to treat a variety of ailments, seen in the names "doctor's root" and "father of health."

(Note: this is *not* a recommendation to use mandrake in your practice, but just an example of what the folk names can tell us about plants. Mandrake is actually highly toxic and also fairly rare, making it an impractical choice for magical work.)

The main problem with common names is that they can vary from region to region especially when it comes to lesser-known plants. One person's "bluebell" may be another person's "witch's thimble" and another's "wild hyacinth." So when researching or shopping for plants, it's best to pay attention to the plant's scientific name, as this will be the name universally recognized across all regions and languages.

Scientific names identify plants based on their physical characteristics. These names are in Latin, and designate the genus and species of the plant. Spike lavender, for example, is known as *Lavandula latifolia*, while English lavender (also called "true lavender") is *Lavandula angustifolia*. If you see just one Latin word followed by the abbreviation *spp.* (as in *Lavandula spp.*) this refers to multiple species within the genus.

Working with plants you've grown or gathered yourself adds an unparalleled richness to your magic. Spells, charms, teas, and other magical workings are always more potent when they're created from your own homegrown resources.

This doesn't mean that you can't work with purchased herbs, flowers, or other ingredients. A full-on homesteading approach to green magic often isn't practical in our modern world. That said, do what you can to incorporate plants into your life, even if it's just a potted herb or two. There's magical reward in simply participating directly with nature's divine intelligence.

GATHERING PLANTS IN THE WILD

Wild harvesting is the most ancient practice in the history of witchcraft. Before humans settled into places where they could cultivate their own herbs, vegetables, and fruits, all plant foods and medicines were foraged in the wild.

Today, wild harvesting is more of a pastime than a necessity, as we can find many of the herbs we work with in natural foods shops or from witchy online merchants, and many green witches may not live in places where foraging is safe and accessible. For example, plants harvested from roadsides may be too contaminated with pollutants to be suitable for medicinal or culinary use. Still, if you get the opportunity, this is definitely a skill worth learning.

The most important thing to know before heading into the wild is how to identify the plants you want to gather and which plants to avoid. As stated in Chapter 1, you should never touch a plant you're not familiar with. While toxic plants are unlikely to kill you just from skin contact, you can end up with stings, blisters, and itchy rashes from a number of common plants in the wild.

Learn to identify poison ivy, oak, and sumac, as well as wild parsnip and giant hogweed. Also keep an eye out for stinging nettles. This powerful herb is well worth gathering if you want to work with it for protection magic or for medicinal teas, but wear gloves and long sleeve shirts and pants. (They will lose their sting once cut and washed.)

(Pro tip: if you ever find yourself feeling frustrated or angry when you're working outdoors with plants, whether gathering in the wild or weeding in the garden, take caution. The fiery energy of poison ivy is attracted to this energy and you may end up bumping up against it unawares!)

You can find help with identifying plants online, but you might also want to have a physical copy of a good field guide to the local flora in your area. There are also a number of apps that allow upload a photo of any plant for instant identification, although these are not always 100% accurate.

It's also a good idea to be aware of any endangered plant species that are either illegal, or simply unethical, to harvest in your area. For example, some species of cacti and wild orchid are either threatened or endangered, as is wild ginseng in many parts of North America. Finally, avoid over-harvesting—take only what you need. And always leave plenty of blooming flowers for the bees and other pollinators, who are essential to the co-creation of healthy ecosystems.

HARMONIOUS HARVESTING

For a sensitive green witch who understands that plants are conscious beings in their own right, harvesting can be a bit of a conundrum, whether we're gathering in the wild, or working with plants we've grown ourselves.

If plants energetically register harmful actions (and even harmful thoughts!) as we saw in Chapter 2, then what happens to the magical energy of a living plant that's being attacked by a knife or a pair of scissors? Is it possible for the disturbances the plant experiences to affect the magical work?

In a word, yes, if the cutting is done clumsily or thoughtlessly. It's important to maintain a respectful attitude and an energy of reverence when cutting into any plant. Thank the plant for sharing its gifts with you. Many witches will leave offerings, such as those suggested in Chapter 5, to plants they harvest in the wild, especially when working with trees. (You'll find more on harvesting from trees in Chapter 8.)

When it comes to plants you tend yourself, you will be establishing a relationship with them based on mutual benefit, and most herbs benefit from regular pruning anyway. Still, it's wise to thank your garden plants when you harvest from them, rather than mindlessly snipping away. You can still give them a little water as an offering (or organic fertilizer, if that will benefit them) at this time.

On a related note, if you're working with fresh herbs bought at a farmer's market or grocery store, you can still thank the spirit of the plant that your herbs came from, which will make your magic (as well as your cooking!) more potent.

THE GREEN WITCH'S GARDEN

Whether your garden is an expanse of diversely planted beds in your yard, or a humble row of pots in your windowsill, or somewhere in between, the experience of growing plants yourself is a gift that every green witch deserves.

Fostering the growing process and reaping the results of your own effort can really deepen your connection to the spiritual energies of the plant. Nurture your magical garden with positive energy, and you will be nurturing yourself at the same time. Both you and your plants will benefit from this co-creative relationship.

MAGICAL HERBS AND FLOWERS FOR POTS, PLANTERS, AND BEDS

Most of the plants discussed here can be grown individually in pots, with other plants in planters, or in raised or in-ground garden beds. Some of the herbs and many of the flowers are annuals, which live out their entire life cycle in one growing season. Perennial herbs and flowers go dormant during the winter and will resume growing in the spring. How to care for perennials in winter will depend on the species, and whether they're potted or in a garden bed. Do some research into the plants that interest you to determine which are best suited for your living situation.

Most herbs and flowers are relatively easy to grow. Vegetables, on the other hand, can get a little more complicated, and are outside the scope of this book. However, if you've got the space, you might also try your hand at growing beginner-friendly foods with magical energies like tomatoes (love, health), green beans (money, abundance), and peppers (creativity, strength). Used in your kitchen, these home-grown beauties will add extra fresh and nutritious magic to any meal, especially when paired with some of your magical herbs (or even some edible flowers!).

MAGICAL HERBS

By and large, the herbs listed here are relatively easy to grow. In addition to their magical properties, all of them have medicinal and culinary uses (yes, even mugwort and yarrow are used by some in soups and other recipes!). Most are suitable for growing in pots, with the exception of mugwort and yarrow, which would require larger pots than is practical for most people. All can be used in magical teas, bath blends, and infused oils, though some are more fragrant than others.

When it comes to harvesting your herbs, researching each species will give you an idea of how much is ideal to take at one time, and how often to do so. Keep in mind that methods will differ from herb to herb. Basil leaves can be easily pinched off with your fingers, for example, while rosemary has heartier stems that require kitchen scissors or garden shears.

Basil (_Omicum basilicum_)

An annual plant, basil is easy to grow and makes an excellent culinary and magical herb. Magical uses: love, luck, wealth, happiness, harmony, courage, fertility, protection of the home.

Chamomile (_Matricaria recutita_)

One of the nine sacred herbs in Anglo-Saxon traditional witchcraft, chamomile has feathery leaves and sweet-smelling flowers that resemble small daisies. Wonderful for teas and scented sachets. Magical uses: healing, stress reduction, peaceful sleep, purification, love, money.

Lavender (_Lavandula angustifolia_)

A very fragrant, calming herb with purple, white, and/or blue flowers blooming at the tops of the plant. Magical uses: love, peace, restful sleep, clairvoyance, happiness, healing, money, passion, protection, relief from grief, longevity, meditation.

Lemon balm (_Melissa officinalis_)

This fragrant and cheerful herb is great for attracting bees to your garden. Lemon balm can get invasive, however, so grow in pots or thin out regularly in planters and beds. Magical uses: healing, fertility, success, love, joy, compassion, clearing negativity, clear thinking, protection.

Mint (_Mentha spp_)

Pots are a good choice for this enthusiastic grower, which is known to take over garden beds and yards. Magical uses: dreamwork (positive dreams), dissolving obstacles, purification, healing, luck, love.

Mugwort (_Artemisia vulgaris_)

A favorite of witches, mugwort grows tall (up to 6 feet), so is not suited for pots. It also needs to be fenced off under the soil to prevent its roots from taking over the rest of the yard. *DO NOT INGEST IF PREGNANT. Magical uses: psychic abilities, dream work, prophetic dreaming, divination, protection of the home and during travel.

Rosemary (_Rosmarinus officinalis_)

A fragrant herb that resembles lavender in appearance, but not in scent. Wonderful for cooking and for eliminating negative vibrations from the home. Magical uses: healing, protection, love, lust, retaining youth, combating jealousy, strengthening mental clarity and focus, promotes good sleep.

Sage (_Salvia officinalis_)

Sage's Latin name, "salvia," comes from the Latin word meaning "to heal. Another powerful culinary and magical herb and one of the hardiest perennials in the bunch. Magical uses: longevity, wisdom, mental clarity, protection, dispelling negative energy (as a smudge), healing energies of grief and loss.

Yarrow (_Achillea millefolium_)

A pretty and powerful medicinal herb, yarrow doesn't taste great in teas, but its healing and magical properties are worth adding extra honey to any magical brew involving this plant. Magical uses: healing, divination, love, courage, protection, psychic receptivity.

MAGICAL FLOWERS

Flowers are used in offerings to nature spirits, in ritual baths, and in many kinds of magical crafts: incense, spell sachets and poppets, flower-infused magical oils, and more. A green witch in the kitchen might use edible flowers in magical potions and culinary spells. Simply having flowers around the home also helps keep the vibrational atmosphere higher, as these are some of nature's most exquisite expressions of divine energy.

Calendula (*Calendula officinalis*)

Calendula is an annual plant with vibrant yellow, orange, and cream flowers and a long blooming season. Be sure to deadhead spent flowers to keep the blooms coming. The flowers are also great for vases. Magical uses: health, wealth, beauty, luck, honoring the deceased.

Geranium (*Geranium spp*)

Geraniums grow well in pots, planters, and beds. They can be overwintered indoors in a sunny location, or stored in a dark, cool place to go dormant until spring. Magical uses: happiness, healing, overcoming negativity, fertility, childbirth, protection.

Marigold (*Tagetes spp*)

Marigolds are great for keeping unwanted pests out of your garden, and can be planted as a first line of defense to protect herbs and vegetables. They also do well in pots, but choose large ones as they need a lot of space. Magical uses: psychic ability, love, protection, healing from grief, honoring ancestors.

Nasturtium (*Tropaeolum majus*)

Nasturtium flowers are as edible as they are cheerful, and will bloom well into the fall. This is a trailing plant, although some varieties are more bush-like. Magical uses: happiness, love, purification, protection, empowerment, inspiration.

Snapdragon (*Antirrhinum majus*)

Distinctive long stalks and clusters of bell-shaped blooms characterize these pollinator-friendly flowers. They bloom in late spring through fall, depending on the climate. If left to go to seed, snapdragons will return in your garden bed the following spring. Magical uses: protection, repelling negative energy, purification, clear thinking, strength.

Sunflower (*Helianthus gracilentus*)

Yes, you can grow sunflowers in pots, provided they're the dwarf variety. The seeds and petals are easy to harvest for magical work, and the seeds are edible. Magical uses: success, good health, happiness, wisdom, positive energy, growth, abundance.

Violet (*Viola spp*)

There are hundreds of species of this dainty flower, including annuals and perennials. Violets typically grow best in partial shade. They are difficult to grow indoors, but do well in outdoor pots and planters. Magical uses: protection, love, restful sleep, tranquility, harmony, luck.

MAGICAL GARDENING TIPS

If you do a basic internet search on nearly any question you have about a specific plant, or about gardening in general, you'll likely find an overwhelming amount of information. From books to blogs to video tutorials, there's a wide array of advice at your fingertips, coming from professional gardeners and amateur enthusiasts alike.

This is an excellent way to find ideas, inspirations, and solutions for all kinds of plant problems. Once you dive in a bit, however, you'll also find plenty of conflicting information and advice. This can be frustrating, but keep in mind that various environmental and climate factors, as well as differing species of plants, can impact the effectiveness of any plant care approach.

Do take advantage of expert advice, and keep the following recommendations in mind, but also remember that personal, hands-on experience will always be your best teacher.

Start small. If you're brand-new to gardening, don't try to go all-out in the first growing season. You might be eager to plant 10 different herbs and flowers or create a raised vegetable bed right away, but it's important not to set yourself up for overwhelm. Choose a few beginner-friendly plants to start with, and focus on what you learn from tending them. If growing from seeds is more than you're ready to take on, get some established starter plants instead. Then you'll be well set up for expanding your garden over time.

Let the philosophy of permaculture be a guiding principle.
We saw in Chapter 2 how working co-creatively with nature, rather than against it, brings positive results. Strive

to support nature's divine intelligence by using regenerative strategies in your garden. Plant pollinator-friendly herbs and flowers, use only natural pesticides and fungicides (and only if needed). Unlike wild nature, where many different species will return nutrients to the soil in the form of decomposition, gardens require a bit of help to maintain healthy soil. Use compost, organic fertilizer, and other organic soil amendments to give your garden the best, and to get the best out of your garden. And wherever possible, purchase seeds and plant starts from local sources.

Create faerie space in your garden. Taking good care of your plants will already endear you to nature spirits, but you can take it a step further by consciously inviting the faeries to visit your magical space. Plant traditional fairy flowers like columbine, foxglove, or violets, and leave a bowl of small crystals or shiny stones near them. Inscribe magical symbols on your pots and planters. Adorn your indoor plants with decorative stakes or place crystals in the soil (more on this in Chapter 8). There are many ways to attract faerie energy—the key component is using your own natural creativity!

Know when (and how much) to water. Plants have varying water needs, so it's a good idea to research the ideal conditions for each type of plant you're growing. Generally speaking, most flowers have similar water needs, with more variance among vegetables and herbs. Annual plants need more water than established perennials.

Spend time in your garden. Make a point of checking on your plants often—at least once a day during critical times, such as the first few weeks after planting seeds or during hot, dry stretches. This will help you spot any problems early on, like bugs or wildlife critters snacking on your plants, and monitor their water needs. It also strengthens your intuitive connection to your plants and your garden as a whole—again, whether your garden is outside or in pots on a window sill.

Talk to your plants. As we saw in Chapter 2, plants are sensitive beyond our imagination, and they will respond positively to positive intentions sent their way. They may not understand spoken language, but they do translate vibrational frequency, and are more likely to thrive when consciously acknowledged in a loving manner.

Be patient with nature, and with yourself. Growing plants is a fairly simple and straightforward process, yet there's also an element of trial and error. You are going to make mistakes, and you might sometimes accidentally kill your plants, but this is how we learn. Even experienced gardeners still have challenges in the quest to co-create harmoniously with nature. Approach your magical garden with a spirit of adventure and experimentation, and don't let any initial failures get you down.

DRYING AND STORING HERBS

When you need herbs for a recipe or a spell, nothing beats simply grabbing a pair of kitchen scissors and heading out to your garden. However, this is not a year-round option, unless you live in a tropical region. Harvesting and drying your fresh herbs (and flowers) makes them available outside of the growing season. Dried herbs and flowers can also be easier to manage in spellwork and magical crafting.

The most traditional way to dry herbs is to hang them in bunches upside down in a dry, well-ventilated place away from direct sunlight. Most herbs take about three weeks to dry completely, to the point where the leaves crack when pinched. (Resist the temptation to take them down before they reach this stage, or you run the risk of mold setting in.)

If you live in a humid climate without air conditioning, it may not be possible to get a completely dry herb using this method, but running a fan might help. You can also place small amounts of herbs upside down in paper bags, which will absorb some of the plants' moisture. Just don't overcrowd the bag, and check on the herbs regularly.

If hanging isn't possible, or you just don't want to wait long to use your dried herbs, there's always the oven. Used on the lowest setting, ovens take just a couple of hours to dry most herbs, and even less time for flower petals. Simply lay them flat on a baking sheet lined with parchment paper, and check on them frequently to avoid burning them.

Herbs will lose more of their flavor and aroma in the oven than if air-dried. Make sure your oven is clean, with no leftover traces of burnt-on food, or your herbs will smell like whatever you last cooked. A dehydrator is another option, if you have one. Many witches delight in using these to dry their herbs and flowers.

For delicate flower petals, air drying is a good way to go, especially if you aren't drying a lot at a time. Use a baking tray or a wide-bottomed bowl to lay them out on paper towels or a clean, lint-free cloth. Check on them daily and stir gently with your fingers to dry them evenly. You can also hang single flowers upside down by their stems to dry them whole.

Store dried herbs and flower petals in glass jars for best results. If this isn't possible, you can use ziplock bags, but make sure they're sealed airtight. Keep all dried plant materials out of direct sunlight and away from consistent heat. Make sure you label everything, and include the date so you'll know how old the herbs are as time passes. Don't skip this step—it always feels like we'll remember which herb we put where, but weeks and months down the line, you'll be glad you made it easy on yourself!

GARDENING WITH THE MOON

Gardening and farming according to lunar phases is rooted in age-old folklore, as our ancestors observed the moon's effects on their crops. Obviously, people with busy schedules may not be able to strictly adhere to the framework suggested here, and that's fine. But when possible, working with the lunar cycle brings a "green thumb" effect to your efforts!

These guidelines are mostly focused around outdoor vegetable and herb gardens. If you're working strictly with potted herbs and flowers, or if all of your outdoor plants are of the same type, you can still tend them according to the basic patterns of waxing and waning: plant, fertilize, and gently weed during the waxing phase, and prune, harvest, and transplant during the waning.

First Quarter (New to waxing Half): This is the best time to plant above-ground crops that produce seeds outside of the fruit, such as grain crops, broccoli and other cruciferous vegetables, spinach and other greens, and most annual herbs.

Second Quarter (waxing Half to Full): Plant above-ground crops that produce their seeds inside the fruit or seed pod, such as beans, tomatoes, peppers, and squash. The two to three days before the Full Moon are the "sweet spot" for planting during this period.

Third Quarter (Full to waning Half): As the waning phase begins, particularly in the first few days after the Full Moon, the time is perfect for planting root vegetables like carrots, potatoes, beets and onions. Bulbs, perennials, and biennials are favored now as well.

Fourth Quarter (waning Half to Dark): This phase is best for weeding, harvesting, pruning, and transplanting crops. Give your houseplants a little extra love at this time as well, and then let everything rest—yourself included!—for a few days before the New Moon.

CHAPTER SEVEN
CREATING SACRED SPACE

HARMONIZE YOUR LIVING SPACE WITH NATURE'S ENERGIES

No matter what your living situation, whether you have an apartment all your own or just a small room, it's very beneficial to create some sacred space for yourself. "Sacred space" simply means an energetic refuge from the outside world, where you can connect with yourself and focus on your spiritual path. Whether this is an altar, a corner of a room, an entire room, or an entire house depends on your preferences and circumstances, but the ideas presented in this chapter can be applied to any space you inhabit.

Most of us today are at least a little familiar with the ancient Chinese practice of feng shui. The term "feng shui" literally translates to "wind-water," pointing to the natural energy that interacts with all physical reality on Earth. This tradition recognizes that a given space can be deliberately arranged to promote the harmonious flow of energy throughout that space.

Green witches are also attuned to energy at this level, whether through studying and applying feng shui principles, or through simply using their intuition to foster harmonious energy in their homes. One approach is to bring in objects from nature that embody the energies of the four elements, as we saw in Chapter 3, to promote a balanced atmosphere.

You can also hang artwork depicting elemental manifestations, such as trees, flowers, waterfalls, or anything that brings you joy to look at. Pottery is a great way to bring the earth element into your decor. The air element can be incorporated through simmering potpourri blends, burning incense, or heating essential oils in a diffuser.

Additionally, you can place seasonal items on your altar (or elsewhere in your space), like flowers, autumn leaves, and evergreen boughs. This practice is a good way to remind yourself to change things up every so often, as even the most harmoniously arranged space can begin to feel flat after awhile. From time to time, you may find that an elegant tree branch or a crow feather shows up right on your path, signaling that it would bring good energy into your home, if even just for a short stay.

Of course, plants are the ideal natural companions for enhancing the spiritual atmosphere of any space, as are crystals. Both of these are discussed in further detail, below. But lest you get overwhelmed with the possibilities for designing your own green witch's refuge, know that it's fine to start small, and let your sacred space be a continual work in progress.

MAGICAL PLANT COMPANIONS

Houseplants unquestionably improve the energy of your living space, as well as your physical, mental, and emotional well-being. Studies have shown that people with plants in their indoor environments experienced reduced stress, increased creativity and productivity, and even lower blood pressure. While scientists may not be able to point to the exact reasons for these effects, witches know that these are examples of nature's divine intelligence at work. As a bonus, plants can be incorporated into spaces you share with non-witches, without raising any eyebrows.

Like outdoor gardening, tending indoor plants is a hands-on education in the dynamics of light, water, soil, and non-physical energy. Different plants require different growing conditions. Some are fairly high-maintenance, while others actually prefer to be ignored much of the time. Many plants need a lot of sunlight, but some thrive in low light, and there are even plants that survive on air alone!

Anyone can keep at least a plant or two, regardless of where they live or the size of their living space. With a little research and some intuitive receptivity, you can find the right plants for your situation. Here are some excellent, relatively low-maintenance plants you might start with:

Aloe (*Aloe vera*)

A potent magical and medicinal plant, the protective nature of this bright green succulent keeps negative energy at bay and helps ward against household accidents, especially in the kitchen. The gel stored in aloe leaves has been used since ancient times to heal burns and other skin problems, and to promote healthy digestion. It's also used in spellwork related to health, beauty, love, and abundance. Aloe needs a fair amount of sunlight to thrive. Water it deeply but infrequently—only when the top inch or so of the soil is dry.

Jade plant (*Crassula ovata*)

Another delightful succulent, jade is named for its thick deep green leaves that resemble jade stone. Also known as "money tree," jade attracts abundance and wealth, and is magically associated with luck, health, and friendship. Jade likes bright, indirect light, but can also tolerate relatively low light. Like aloe, jade can be easily overwatered, so allow the soil to dry before giving it a good soak, and never let the roots sit in water.

Pothos (*Epipremnum aureum*)

This unruly yet elegant trailing vine with heart-shaped leaves is the perfect low-maintenance plant. It can be hung in baskets or trained to climb up walls and windowsills. Incredibly resilient, pothos can tolerate low light and will survive without consistent watering, though it will grow better if kept consistently moist. It's also very easy to propagate from cuttings, so you can create multiple plants rather quickly. Pothos removes negative energy and pollutants from the home. Its magical properties include protection, resilience, and forgiveness.

Spider plant (*Chlorophytum comosum*)

Spider plant has long, narrow leaves resembling blades of grass with white stripes. They reproduce by shooting out baby plants that resemble spiders dangling from webs. Another good hanging plant, this is a great option for spaces without a lot of direct sunlight. Let them dry substantially (but not completely) between waterings. Spider plants purify the home and absorb negativity, and carry energies of protection, wisdom, healing, and (when baby plants are present) fertility.

Money tree (*Pachira aquatica*)

Not to be confused with jade plant, this small palm-like tree can grow up to 6 feet indoors, but can be kept pruned to smaller heights. Money tree is typically sold with braided stems, meaning two or more plants are potted together and braided into one big "trunk." Magically, money tree is associated with wealth, of course, but also balance (which is often a root aspect of money issues!) and friendship. It's a go-to in feng shui traditions for attracting luck, positive energy, and prosperity.

African violet (*Saintpaulia ionantha*)

An excellent flowering addition to your indoor garden, African violet is not a true violet, but is named for its blooms in many shades of blue, violet, pink, and white. With sufficient warmth, humidity, and indirect sunlight, African violets can bloom year round. They may need more regular monitoring than other houseplants, but are generally easy to care for. Associated with the moon and the water element, African violet is a great plant to have on or near your altar, especially for spellwork involving love, spiritual quests, and protection.

Air plants (*Tillandsia spp*)

There are more than 600 species of tillandsia, with widely varying appearances. Spanish moss, which has long been used in Afro-Cuban and hoodoo magic, is one example. Air plants are epiphytes, meaning they don't grow in soil. Instead, they attach to rocks, tree branches, or other surfaces and take their nutrients from the moisture in the air. They are watered through misting or soaking, depending on the species. Most can tolerate low light conditions. Magically, air plants support patience and a calm atmosphere. As quintessential plants of the air element, they're great to keep anywhere you work or study.

Keep in mind that plenty of plants are safe for humans but toxic to pets, so be sure to check for toxicity before bringing a new plant into your home. Of the plants described here, aloe, jade, and pothos are considered toxic to pets, while spider plant, money tree, African violet, and tillandsia are widely regarded as safe.

"GREEN THUMB" ADVICE FOR HOUSE PLANTS

Here are a few strategies for a successful indoor green witch garden:

• Research the specific light requirements of the plants that interest you so you'll know whether they're a good fit for your space. You'll also want to know what kind of soil they need once it comes time to repot them. As for "plant food," which is actually fertilizer, indoor plants don't really need it, but it's an option if you want them to grow more rapidly during the spring and summer.

- Be sure to also look up the plant's watering needs, as these can vary widely. Make a point of checking your plants' water levels regularly, but avoid the temptation to water everything at once for the sake of convenience. Overwatering can cause as many problems as not watering enough.

- Consider making a ritual out of watering your plants. You can magically charge the water itself with a spoken blessing, and even add a quartz crystal to the water a few hours before using it.

- As with your garden plants, talk to your houseplants. Let them know you appreciate them and want them to thrive.

- Also recognize that your plants talk to you through their behavior. If they're wilting or turning brown or yellow, they need something from you. If all of your plants are struggling, it may even be a sign that an energetic clearing is in order, either of your home or yourself, or both.

As with outdoor gardening, there's an element of trial and error when it comes to tending indoor plants. Don't be discouraged if you find that a plant doesn't thrive once you've brought it home. Just consider it a learning opportunity, do some research to identify potential causes of the problem, and try again.

CRYSTALS: BRINGING EARTH ENERGIES INTO YOUR HOME

As products of nature's divine intelligence, crystals and other mineral stones are reservoirs and transmitters of a wide spectrum of beneficial energies. While they may be technically inorganic materials, Witches understand that crystals are as "alive" as any plant or animal, from an energetic perspective. They will have subtle but noticeable effects anywhere you place them in your space.

Crystal grids, created with multiple stones in geometric patterns, amplify the power of individual stones and create an energetic field throughout the area of the grid. You can place jet and/ or amethyst in each corner of a room (or house) for example, for protection and/or a calm atmosphere.

You can also simply keep crystals on your altar, desk, tables and other furniture. Line a windowsill with sunlight-tolerant stones, or arrange small polished stones in an attractive clay bowl. Crystals and stones are easy and fun to get creative with. Here are a few delightful suggestions with beneficial energies for your space:

Quartz crystal (clear/white)

Clear quartz crystal dispels negative energy from other people in your environment and restores positive energy to people and places. A good stone for concentration, memory, psychic ability, and communication with animals and plants. It's also a good meditation stone.

Rose quartz (pink)

Rose quartz has a gentle, nurturing energy that promotes harmony and emotional healing. Place it by your bed for peaceful sleep, under a child's pillow to stop nightmares, or by your computer to help prevent eye fatigue and headaches.

Carnelian (red/orange)

The energy of carnelian is bold and joyful, but also has a grounding influence. It's a good stone for motivation, courage, and endurance. It also has protective energies. Some people use it to guard their homes from theft, storms, fires, or other damage.

Citrine (yellow)

Citrine is known as the "sun stone." It can brighten up a space (or your mood) with its ability to instantly transmute negative energy into positive energy. A good crystal for creativity, self-expression, and self-confidence. Place it in prominent locations where you'll see it often.

Malachite (green)

Malachite is a stone of spiritual transformation and is a great ally when dealing with big changes. It also helps protect from too much psychic energy in crowded places. Malachite can also dispel energetic toxins from fluorescent lighting, electrical equipment, and unwanted noise.

Lapis lazuli (blue)

A very spiritual stone, lapis lazuli helps maintain contact with the higher self. It's a good stone for inspiration, communication, easing depression, and restoring inner peace. Keep one on your altar or in your sacred space to enhance psychic ability and access the spiritual plane.

Amethyst (violet)

Amethyst has a very high vibration, and will contribute to maintaining a positive atmosphere anywhere it is placed. It's a great crystal for creativity, focus, and imagination. It also helps balance addictive behaviors. Place under your pillow for restful sleep, and near your computer to help relieve eye strain.

Jet (black)

Jet is actually fossilized driftwood. Having begun as one substance and ended as another, it's a helpful stone for transitions. Jet absorbs energy from negative thoughts. It's used to protect the home from unwanted energies and psychic vampires. Some witches find it a good all-around enhancer of magical work.

Moonstone (white/pale blue/grey)

Moonstone is another good sleep stone, especially for children. Its affinity with the moon makes it a strong stone for wisdom and psychic ability. Traditionally a stone of safe travels, it is said to help guard against road rage and accidents when kept in the glove compartment.

When choosing crystals, focus on just feeling the energies of each stone and noticing which ones resonate with you on an intuitive level. Magical associations are useful to keep in mind, but it's more important to choose colors, textures, and other characteristics that call to you. Place them where they seem to "want" to go, and move them around from time to time when you feel the space needs a change. This is working with Earth's intelligence at its finest.

CLEARING AND BLESSING YOUR SACRED SPACE

If you're revamping the energy of your space for the first time, this ritual is an excellent way to seal and activate the work. However, because our personal energies change and morph over time as we experience life, the sacred space we inhabit requires some regular energetic maintenance. You might choose to repeat this ritual (or one of your own design) at each equinox, each full moon, or any time you feel the energy of your space has become stale or stagnant.

Clearing:

Sweep (or vacuum) the floor(s) to remove physical manifestations of the old energy. Then smudge with sage, cedar, lavender, juniper, and/or other cleansing herbs to purify the air and clear out unwanted nonphysical energy. If burning herbs is not an option, use a purification essential oil blend in an oil burner or diffuser (see Chapter 8 for an example recipe). Or, infuse a dish of water with protective herbs and/or crystals and sprinkle it around the floors with a sprig of rosemary, lavender, pine needles, or cedar leaves. It's important to open at least one window for a few moments after this step, so the energy has somewhere to go.

Blessing:

Briefly burn sweetgrass, incense (such as copal), or essential oil (such as lemon) that bring light and positive energy into your space. Alternatively (or additionally), you can anoint the windows and doorways of the space with a blessing oil (see Chapter 8 for an example recipe). When you're finished, take a deep breath and spend a moment appreciating your space and everything in it. Say thank you, silently or aloud, to the energy of the space and the refuge it provides for you.

After the ritual, it's nice to step outside, go for a walk, or otherwise vacate the space for a little while. Then when you return, take a moment to notice the change in the energy.

CHAPTER EIGHT
SPELLS, RECIPES, AND MAGICAL INSPIRATIONS

PRACTICAL MAGIC FOR THE GREEN WITCH

Whether you're new to magic or a seasoned witch, this brief collection of magical information is just a starting off point for further explorations of the green path of witchcraft.

Here, you'll find a few magical workings, correspondences for common spell ingredients, recipe inspirations for teas, magical oils, and incense, and more.

ENERGIZE YOUR MAGICAL ALLIES

Whether you're working with ingredients you've gathered or grown yourself, or herbs you found at the grocery store, it's important to charge them for magical work. If you've purchased or received the item from someone else, be sure to clear any lingering energies before proceeding.

Sage or other purifying herbs or an asperging water (see Chapter 7) work well for denser energies, while items needing just a little clearing can be left out in sunlight or moonlight for several hours. (Note: translucent crystals fade in the sun, so research first.) Anything you've grown or gathered in the wild is already clear and ready to charge.

"Charging" is really the act of linking up on both the physical and spiritual planes with the energies inherent in the herbs, crystals, and other allies you work with. Formally confirming this connection with a ritual action seals the work. One simple way is to hold the item in your hands and visualize your own personal power flowing through them into the item. If you feel called to, you can say the following (or similar) words:

"I give thanks for this [item] and empower it for [name your purpose]."

Clearing and charging can be done at any point before ritual or spellwork begins. You can charge herbs right after you harvest them, if using them fresh, or after they're dried, if preserving them for long-term use. If you're creating a magical craft, you can charge the finished product at the end of the spell. Follow your intuition regarding methods and timing, but do take the time for this important step.

TREE MAGIC

Witches and other spiritual practitioners have known for millennia that trees are powerful magical allies. Trees emit powerful energies that affect everything around them, and even scientists have discovered that simply spending time near trees can result in improved focus, stress reduction, and better emotional health.

Not everyone has direct access to trees in their environment, but you can still connect with their energies by visiting parks and forests when possible, and by working with the gifts they provide us in magic.

For green witches who use wands, nothing beats a perfect length of branch from a willow, birch, hazel, or other beloved tree. In spellwork, green witches may work with a tree's bark, branches, leaves, flowers, fruits, or nuts. Acorns, pinecones, apple seeds, blossom petals, holly berries, autumn leaves—anything a tree produces can be used in magic of all kinds. Plenty of magical online retailers offer spell ingredients from trees, if you aren't able to access them on your own.

Many trees contain aromatic properties that make for wonderfully rich essential oils with potent magical energies. For example:

- **Birch** ("sweet birch"): purification, healing, fertility
- **Cedar** ("cedarwood"): banishing, good health, connection with divine energy
- **Fir:** prosperity, vitality, winter solstice rituals
- **Pine:** purification, banishing, fertility

Some trees are also used in smudges and incense:

- **Cedar:** burn cedar smudge wands or loose cedar bark chips to purify and consecrate sacred space
- **Oak:** burn chips of oak bark for prosperity and/or use it as a base for an incense blend
- **Pine:** burn the needles for purification, healing, and to attract money.
- **Rowan:** burn dried leaves, bark, or berries for protection and to increase psychic awareness

Many green witches prefer to avoid harvesting anything from a living tree, instead using only leaves, bark, branches or fruits that have already dropped to the ground. If you do choose to harvest from a living tree, you'll need to research the individual species for to do so with minimal damage to the tree. Never cut bark directly from the trunk, pull leaves off by their stems, or use gardening shears, as all of these actions can hinder healing and future growth. And always connect energetically with the spirit of the tree first, and respectfully ask permission to remove anything.

Whether you're harvesting or just gathering from the ground, it's good to bring an offering for the tree as an energetic exchange for what it has shared with you. Flowers, a small crystal, or a few drops of water, milk, or honey are good choices, but as always, go with your intuition.

NATURE'S BOUNTY ABUNDANCE JAR

This magical creation both celebrates and attracts more of the abundance provided to us through nature's divine intelligence. Any of the ingredients can be substituted with other herbs, flowers, seeds, etc. with money, abundance, or prosperity associations, so feel free to create your own version of this recipe according to what you have on hand, or can gather locally.

Try to incorporate a wide variety of items, to reflect the diversity of ways that abundance shows up in our lives. Make sure all plant matter is dried before using, to avoid the mixture getting moldy.

You will need:

- 1 work candle for atmosphere
- 1 small wide-mouthed jar with screw-top lid
- Mortar & pestle (or bowl and spoon)
- Several tablespoons honey or maple syrup (enough to fill the jar)

- 1-3 tablespoons of each of the following:
  - basil
  - chamomile
  - lavender
- 8 sunflower seeds
- Several petals from calendula, coneflower, and/or honeysuckle
- Crushed leaves, seeds, and/or bark from maple, oak, cedar, fir, and/or pine
- 1 piece bloodstone, citrine, jade, malachite, or tiger's eye
- 3-5 drops patchouli, bergamot, or lavender essential oil (or a blend of these)

Instructions:

Light the candle and take a few deep, centering breaths. Bring the concept of abundance into your awareness, and take time to acknowledge any and all abundance in your life at this moment (regardless of how it might measure up to what you want to experience!)

Add the dried plant materials to the mortar (or bowl) one at a time, and mix the together with the pestle (or spoon). Then use your fingers to mix them further, infusing the plants' energies with your own personal energy.

Next, place the crystal in the jar, envisioning it as a magnet that draws abundance to you. Cover the stone with the plant mixture, then add the drops of oil. Pour the honey over the mixture until it reaches the top of the jar.

Seal the jar with the lid and hold it in your hands for a few moments, visualizing the abundance flowing into your life. If you like, say the following (or similar) words:

"As nature eternally creates and renews, so the bounty of abundance in my life is assured."

Place the jar in direct sunshine to charge for several hours. Then keep it on your altar, in your kitchen, or in another prominent place to remind you of the abundance you currently have and will continue to attract into your life.

Eventually you will sense that the energy of the jar is no longer active. When this happens, bury the contents in the earth (or compost the organic matter and bury the crystal), giving thanks for the abundance in your life as you do so. Rinse and recycle the jar.

CHARM FOR ADAPTING TO CHANGE

As discussed in Chapter 4, change is necessary for growth and manifestation to occur, but that doesn't mean it's always comfortable, even when it's wanted. Whether you're navigating changes in relationship, a job, or the world at large), the energies of this charm can help you stay balanced and open to the positive developments that can come your way as a result of the change.

The herbs and fir needles for this spell can be fresh or dried. Fresh plant matter will be more pungent, but will not last as long.

You will need:

- Small white, blue, or violet candle (preferably beeswax, soy, or candelilla wax)
- Small drawstring bag
- 1 piece malachite
- Small piece of shed willow bark

- Fir needles
- Sage leaves
- Thyme leaves
- A few drops palmarosa essential oil
- Journal or writing paper (optional)

<u>Instructions:</u>

Light the candle, and spend a few moments freewriting (or just reflecting) on the change(s) you're dealing with at the moment. Identify any aspects that you need help accepting, or concerns you have about what comes next. Then identify how you want to feel once you've adjusted to the change. Hold this feeling in your mind as you begin the work.

Mix the leaves, bark and needles in a mortar or bowl with your fingers infusing the plants' energies with your own personal energy. Add the mixture to the drawstring bag, and sprinkle a few drops of the oil onto the malachite and add it to the bag. Close up the bag and place it in front of the candle to charge. Seal the work with the following (or similar) words:

"As each day moves forward, I learn to walk my path in this new reality. I trust that the divine intelligence of the universe will lead me through. And so it is."

Leave the candle to burn out on its own, or for several hours before gently extinguishing it. Keep the charm near you as much as possible until you feel yourself finding equilibrium again.

CRYSTALS FOR GARDENS AND HOUSEPLANTS

Just as crystals can enhance the atmosphere of a space or promote healing of the mind, body, and spirit, their healing energies are beneficial to plant life. Crystals and other mineral stones can be placed on or within the soil in gardens and potted plants.

Some are beneficial to root growth and can be buried at the bottom of pots or at the root level in a garden bed. Many can also be used to create an elixir for watering plants (as mentioned in Chapter 7). Certain crystals will dissolve in water, however, so always research any stone you're unfamiliar with.

Using crystals in this way can also improve your personal connection to your plants, especially stones like moss agate and amethyst. Tiger's eye can even boost your confidence in your own plant-tending abilities. Here are a few to try:

Moss agate is literally known as "the gardener's stone." It promotes healthy plant tissue and strengthens the energetic bond between you and your plants.

Moonstone embodies peaceful, restful energies. It's great for restoring stressed or wilting plants to good health and promoting fertility.

Malachite promotes fertility and abundance and protects against electromagnetic pollution. Raw malachite can deteriorate in water, so polished stones are best.

Citrine embodies solar energy and revitalizes "sad" or sickly plants. It cleanses negative vibrations and infuses your garden with positive energy.

Quartz crystal is known as a "master healer," which applies to plants, too! It brings very high vibrations to houseplants and gardens.

Amethyst is another "master healer," promoting peace and stability. Place it in stressed plants and to protect against electromagnetic pollution.

Tiger's eye promotes strong roots and abundant harvests. Place around the base of potted plants, or bury in the soil at root level.

THE MAGIC OF TEA

Teas make for powerful magic because the herbs interact directly with your physical body. They're also a great way to make use of an herb's medicinal and magical properties at the same time. Teas made from herbs you've grown and dried yourself are extra potent, but you can also find quality herbs from both magical and natural foods shops. When done with the right intention, the act of making tea can be considered a spell in and of itself.

Place loose herbs in a stainless-steel mesh tea ball, or steep them loose and then pour into a new mug through a fine strainer. As you pour the water over the herbs, visualize the benefits you intend the tea to assist with. This could be a fruitful divination session, success with a project, physical or emotional healing, or just simply a relaxing evening—whatever your desire, there's probably a tea for it! Allow the tea to steep for 5 to 10 minutes, depending on your preferred strength. For extra medicinal benefits, cover the mug while steeping.

The best way to learn which herbs work best for you is to experiment, both with single herbs and blends. If an herb is new to you, try it on its own first, before adding other herbs to it. Not all herbs are particularly tasty, so try adding a little honey to balance any bitterness (and add an extra dose of natural goodness to the mix!).

Unless otherwise noted, the herbs below can be used in equal parts to create a blend. For a single cup, ¼ to ½ teaspoon per herb creates an ample serving. Or mix a tablespoon or more per herb and store the blend in a jar. Again, start small—rather than throwing every herb in the list into your blend, try two, then add a third the next time, and so on. While "the more, the merrier" isn't a bad guiding principle here, there's also a lot to be said for simplicity.

Divination and Prophetic Dreams

- mugwort
- dandelion
- chamomile
- yarrow
- cinnamon (use less)
- elecampane (use less: very bitter)

Immunity Enhancers

- echinacea
- hibiscus
- nettle leaf
- elderberry
- lemon balm
- ginger root

Anxiety Banishers

- chamomile
- hibiscus

- peppermint
- lavender
- lemon balm
- passionflower
- valerian

Motivation and Focus

- green teas
- black teas
- ginger
- peppermint
- rosemary
- spearmint
- hibiscus

ESSENTIAL OIL ALLIES

While essential oils are a relatively recent phenomenon, fragrant botanical oils have been around since antiquity. Today, essential oils are often part and parcel of the life of a green witch. They have the same magical properties as the plants they come from, but in even more concentrated form, due to the amount of plants required to produce a small quantity of oil.

Whether used singly or in blends, botanical oils can help soothe frayed nerves, focus the mind, and open us up to the subtle energies of the spiritual plane, where our focused magical intention begins the journey to full manifestation.

If you're new to blending oils, it's helpful to start with recipes until you're familiar enough with the scents to experiment on your own. For oil burners and diffusers, use the oils straight. For anointing oils, use a carrier oil like almond, grapeseed, or jojoba. A general rule of thumb is 2 tablespoons carrier oil for 10-15 drops of essential oil.

Using an eyedropper or the single-drop dispenser included in most essential oil bottles, count out the number of drops called for in the recipe. Be sure to follow the order the ingredients are listed in, as the larger amounts should go into the blend first. Gently swirl the jar around clockwise to mix the oil into the carrier (if using). Sniff the jar as you add each oil, repeat, noticing the difference each makes to the scent of the blend. Let the scents become associated with the purpose of the oil in your mind.

Bright Blessings Oil**

- 4 drops lavender oil
- 3 drops lemon oil
- 2 drops bergamot oil
- 1 drop rose oil

Prosperity Oil*

- 5 drops patchouli
- 2 drops cedarwood
- 1 drop lavender
- 1 drop clove oil

Home Protection Oil*

- 5 drops vetiver
- 2 drops clove
- 1 drop cinnamon
- 1 drop ylang ylang

Purification Oil

- 5 drops juniper
- 3 drops cedarwood

- 2 drops lavender

*For anointing objects, but not skin (clove and cinnamon are skin irritants).
**Do not wear on skin that will be exposed to sunlight.

NATURAL MAGICAL INCENSE

Typically, incense blends involve a variety of ingredients, including herbs, resins, tree barks and resins, and/or essential oils. However, single-ingredient incenses also work well to enhance the energy of your space and create a state of mind conducive to spellwork.

Making your own incense can be a relatively complicated process, depending on the form of the incense (cone, stick/wand, or loose) and how many ingredients you want to include. You can find plenty of instructions for making all kinds of incense, online and in print sources. A detailed breakdown of instructions for each type is beyond the scope of this book, but here are some suggested ingredients for potential blends to inspire your explorations:

Purification

- benzoin
- copal
- myrrh
- sandalwood (wood or oil)
- cedar (shavings or oil)
- clove oil
- birch oil

Protection

- dragon's blood
- gum arabic

- sandalwood (wood or oil)
- oak bark
- juniper (wood, berries, tips, or oil)

Spiritual Connection

- amber
- benzoin
- dragon's blood
- gum arabic
- myrrh
- patchouli (leaves or oil)
- sandalwood (wood or oil)

Peaceful Vibrations

- amber
- copal
- frankincense (resin or oil)
- jasmine (flowers or oil)
- patchouli (leaves or oil)

MAGICAL ASSOCIATIONS OF COMMON HERBS

Herb	Magical Uses
Basil	love, luck, wealth, happiness, harmony, courage, fertility, protection of the home
Bay Leaf	protection, purification, healing, strength, good fortune, money, and success
Chamomile	healing, stress reduction, peaceful sleep, purification, love, money
Dandelion	divination, interaction with the spirit world, wishes
Elecampane	protection, luck, dispels negative vibration, plant spirit communication
Lavender	love, peace, restful sleep, clairvoyance, happiness, healing, money, passion, protection, relief from grief, longevity, meditation
Lemon Balm	healing, fertility, success, love, joy, compassion, clearing negativity, clear thinking, protection
Mint	dreamwork (positive dreams), dissolving obstacles, purification, healing, luck, love
Mugwort	psychic abilities, dream work, prophetic dreaming, divination, protection of the home and during travel
Rosemary	healing, protection, love, lust, retaining youth, combating jealousy, strengthening mental clarity and focus, promotes good sleep
Sage	longevity, wisdom, mental clarity, protection, dispelling negative energy (as a smudge), healing energies of grief and loss
Thyme	purification, courage, emotional healing, honoring the dead, attracting loyalty, abundance, psychic abilities
Valerian	sleep, love, protection from negativity, purification of sacred space, harmony, communication
Yarrow	healing, divination, love, courage, protection, psychic receptivity

MAGICAL ASSOCIATIONS OF COMMON WILDFLOWERS

Flower	Color(s)	Magical Uses
Buttercup	yellow	love, commitment, fertility, fidelity, humility
Columbine	mainly red and yellow	love, feminine power, beauty, courage
Coneflower	yellow, purple	strength, protection from illness, resilience, prosperity
Daisy	mainly white and yellow	youthful energy, joy, love, flirtation, baby blessings
Foxglove	mainly purple; also white, pink, yellow	protection, clairvoyance, communication with faeries
Honeysuckle	white, pink, red, orange, yellow	intuition, psychic ability, prosperity, love, luck
Violet	mainly blue; also white, yellow, purple	protection, love, restful sleep, tranquility, harmony, luck

MAGICAL ASSOCIATIONS OF COMMON TREES

Tree	Magical Uses
Birch	Purification, illumination, beginnings, renewal, love, beauty, protection
Cedar	Renewal, rejuvenation, protection, purification, luck, health, prosperity, banishing
Fir	Healing, regeneration, childbirth, youth, vitality, prosperity, change
Hawthorn	Fertility, purity, marriage, protection, patience, confidence, creativity
Maple	Travel, beauty, love, joy, prosperity, abundance, creativity, communication
Oak	Strength, prosperity, fertility, courage, wisdom, longevity, abundance, truth, protection, good fortune
Pine	Longevity, renewal, health, strength, fertility, prosperity, purification, good fortune, protection
Rowan	Psychic abilities, healing, positivity, protection, strength, power, insight, nature spirits
Willow	Renewal, immortality, healing grief, vitality, lunar magic, change, love, psychic abilities

MAGICAL ASSOCIATIONS OF CRYSTALS AND MINERAL STONES

Crystal	Color(s)	Magical Uses
Amethyst	violet	sharpens mental focus and intuition, clears sacred space
Bloodstone	green with flecks of red/gold	promotes physical healing, fertility, and abundance
Carnelian	red/orange	wards off negative energies, inspires courage
Citrine	yellow	aids self-confidence, renewal, useful dreams
Hematite	silver/gray/shiny black	strengthens willpower and confidence, helps with problem solving
Jade	green with flecks of red/gold	promotes emotional balance, harmony, and wisdom, protects from negativity
Jet	black	supports transitions through grounding and centering, protection from negativity
Lapis Lazuli	blue/dark blue	helps with altered consciousness, meditation, divination
Malachite	green with bands of dark green and black	supports spiritual growth and emotional courage, helpful during big change
Moonstone	white/pale blue	supports intuition and wisdom, psychic receptivity, creativity
Moss Agate	green/light green	promotes grounding, strengthens resolve, supports connection with natural energies
Quartz Crystal	white/clear	promotes healing, clarity, spiritual development
Rose Quartz	pink	promotes emotional healing, love and friendship
Tiger's Eye	brown/tan/gold with bands of black	protection, energy

MAGICAL ASSOCIATIONS OF ESSENTIAL OILS

Oil	Magical Uses
Bergamot	positive energy, confidence, success, prosperity, peace
Cedarwood	healing, rebirth, spirituality, hex reversal, banishing
Cinnamon	psychic awareness, protection, healing, success, love
Clove	protection, courage, wealth, purification, banishing
Juniper	purification, protection, healing, love
Lavender	healing, peace, love, wealth, purification, dissolving anxiety
Lemon	positive energy, healing, longevity, purification, spiritual awareness
Palmarosa	emotional healing, love, transitions, change
Patchouli	love, lust, physical energy, money, prosperity
Peppermint	dreamwork, dissolving obstacles, purification
Rose	love, peace, balance, enhancing beauty
Vetiver	balance, grounding, love, protection from theft, hex reversal
Ylang Ylang	grounding, protection, peace, sex, love

MAGICAL ASSOCIATIONS OF INCENSE (HERBS AND RESINS)

Incense	Magical Uses
Amber	healing, meditation, divination
Benzoin	purification, prosperity, astral projection
Cedarwood	strength, courage, power
Copal	inspiration, attraction, purification, happiness
Dragon's blood	courage, exorcism, love, magical power, protection
Frankincense	peace, resolving conflict, meditation
Gum arabic	protection, money luck, psychic powers, non-romantic love
Jasmine	love, beauty, emotional connection, friendship
Myrrh	consecration, entity removal, protection, purification, spirituality
Patchouli	grounding, attracting joy, money, prosperity
Sandalwood	purification, protection, healing, spiritual awareness

CONCLUSION

Hopefully this book has given you a solid understanding of what the green path of witchcraft is fundamentally about, and the desire to explore it further. To that end, a list of suggested resources is offered on the following pages, where you'll find a wide variety of perspectives on green witchcraft and related topics.

As you grow in your own unique practice, it's my hope that you will find yourself slowing down more in the midst of this often-hectic life, and paying attention to the natural world around you. Go outside. Get dirty. Take note of how you feel after any encounter with nature, whether it's working in the garden, going for a hike, or simply watching birds outside your window. Appreciate everything you can about each season, each phase of the moon, each day in the constant unfolding of your journey.

Finally, remember that when it comes to magic, patience is part of the process. Just as each phase of the growth cycle has its purpose in the overall enterprise of nature, magical manifestation happens in stages. Most often, the initial developments taking place are not visible to the eye, the way a seed takes root under the surface of the soil. And even as the manifestation begins to emerge, it may not immediately be recognized for what it is, just as seedlings typically resemble each other, no matter what kind of plants they become.

The beginnings of our manifestations can be like this—a chance conversation with an acquaintance that turns out to be a tip on a new job possibility, or a run of what seems to be bad luck (a fender bender, a delayed flight) that puts us in the path of our next true love.

Most realized goals can be traced back to a winding chain of actions and events that seemed unrelated or insignificant until the manifestation became clear. This is just nature's process of co-creation at work. Like life itself, the divine intelligence of nature is surprising, mysterious, unpredictable, and on the whole, breathtakingly beautiful.

SUGGESTIONS FOR FURTHER READING

The following list is by no means comprehensive, but will hopefully inspire you to explore more aspects of the green path. Many of the sources here may incorporate other forms of witchcraft as well, reflecting the overlap between what has come to be called "green" witchcraft and other paths. Happy reading!

Andrews, Ted. *Enchantment of the Faerie Realm: Communicate with Nature Spirits and Elementals*. Woodbury, MN: Llewellyn Publications, 2002.

Beyerl, Paul. *A Compendium of Herbal Magic*. Blaine, WA: Phoenix, 1998.

Beyerl, Paul. *The Master Book of Herbalism*. Blaine, WA: Phoenix, 1984.

Blackthorn, Amy. *Blackthorn's Botanical Magic: The Green Witch's Guide to Essential Oils for Spellcraft, Ritual & Healing*. Newburyport, MA: Weiser Books, 2018.

Chamberlain, Lisa. *Wicca Essential Oils Magic: A Beginner's Guide to Working with Magic Oils*. New York: Sterling Ethos, 2022.

Chamberlain, Lisa. *Wicca Herbal Magic: A Beginner's Guide to Herbal Spellcraft*. New York: Sterling Ethos, 2021.

Chamberlain, Lisa. *Wicca Nature Magic: A Beginner's Guide to Working with Nature Spellcraft*. New York: Sterling Ethos, 2022.

Cunningham, Scott. *Cunningham's Encyclopedia of Crystal, Gem, & Metal Magic*. Woodbury, MN: Llewellyn Publications, 1988.

Cunningham, Scott. *Cunningham's Encyclopedia of Magical Herbs*, **2nd ed.** Woodbury, MN: Llewellyn Publications, 2000.

Cunningham, Scott. *The Complete Book of Incense, Oils & Brews*. Woodbury, MN: Llewellyn Publications, 1989.

Dugan, Ellen. *Garden Witchery: Magic from the Ground Up*. Woodbury, MN: Llewellyn Publications, 2013.

Dugan, Ellen. *Garden Witch's Herbal: Green Magick, Herbalism & Spirituality*. Woodbury, MN: Llewellyn Publications, 2009.

Dugan, Ellen. *Herb Magic for Beginners*. Woodbury, MN: Llewellyn Publications, 2006.

Dugan, Ellen. *Natural Witchery: Intuitive, Personal & Practical Magic*. Woodbury, MN: Llewellyn Publications, 2007.

Moura, Ann. *Green Magic: The Sacred Connection to Nature*. Woodbury, MN: Llewellyn Publications, 2002.

Moura, Ann. *Green Witchcraft: Folk Magic, Fairy Lore, & Herb Craft*. Woodbury, MN: Llewellyn Publications, 1996.

Murphy-Hiscock, Arin. *The Green Witch: Your Complete Guide to the Natural Magic of Herbs, Flowers, Essential Oils, and More*. Avon, MA: Adams Media, 2017.

Murphy-Hiscock, Arin. *The Green Witch's Grimoire: Your Complete Guide to Creating Your Own Book of Natural Magic*. Avon, MA: Adams Media, 2020.

Pogacnik, Marko. *Nature Spirits & Elemental Beings: Working with the Intelligence of Nature*. Rochester, VT: Findhorn Press, 2010.

Silvana, Laura. *Plant Spirit Journey*. Woodbury, MN: Llewellyn Publications, 2009.

Whitehurst, Tess. *The Magic of Flowers: A Guide to Their Metaphysical Uses and Properties*. Woodbury, MN: Llewellyn Publications, 2013.

Whitehurst, Tess. *The Magic of Trees: A Guide to Their Sacred Wisdom & Metaphysical Properties*. Woodbury, MN: Llewellyn Publications, 2017.

THREE FREE AUDIOBOOK PROMOTION

Don't forget, you can now enjoy **three audiobooks completely free of charge** when you start a free 30-day trial with Audible.

If you're new to the Craft, *Wicca Starter Kit* contains three of Lisa's most popular books for beginning Wiccans. You can download it for free at:

www.wiccaliving.com/free-wiccan-audiobooks

Or, if you're wanting to expand your magical skills, check out *Spellbook Starter Kit,* with three collections of spellwork featuring the powerful energies of candles, colors, crystals, mineral stones, and magical herbs. Download over 150 spells for free at:

www.wiccaliving.com/free-spell-audiobooks

Members receive free audiobooks every month, as well as exclusive discounts. And, if you don't want to continue with Audible, just remember to cancel your membership. You won't be charged a cent, and you'll get to keep your books!

Happy listening!

MORE BOOKS BY LISA CHAMBERLAIN

Wicca for Beginners: A Guide to Wiccan Beliefs, Rituals, Magic, and Witchcraft

Wicca Book of Spells: A Book of Shadows for Wiccans, Witches, and Other Practitioners of Magic

Wicca Herbal Magic: A Beginner's Guide to Practicing Wiccan Herbal Magic, with Simple Herb Spells

Wicca Book of Herbal Spells: A Book of Shadows for Wiccans, Witches, and Other Practitioners of Herbal Magic

Wicca Candle Magic: A Beginner's Guide to Practicing Wiccan Candle Magic, with Simple Candle Spells

Wicca Book of Candle Spells: A Book of Shadows for Wiccans, Witches, and Other Practitioners of Candle Magic

Wicca Crystal Magic: A Beginner's Guide to Practicing Wiccan Crystal Magic, with Simple Crystal Spells

Wicca Book of Crystal Spells: A Book of Shadows for Wiccans, Witches, and Other Practitioners of Crystal Magic

Tarot for Beginners: A Guide to Psychic Tarot Reading, Real Tarot Card Meanings, and Simple Tarot Spreads

Runes for Beginners: A Guide to Reading Runes in Divination, Rune Magic, and the Meaning of the Elder Futhark Runes

Wicca Moon Magic: A Wiccan's Guide and Grimoire for Working Magic with Lunar Energies

Wicca Wheel of the Year Magic: A Beginner's Guide to the Sabbats, with History, Symbolism, Celebration Ideas, and Dedicated Sabbat Spells

Wicca Kitchen Witchery: A Beginner's Guide to Magical Cooking, with Simple Spells and Recipes

Wicca Essential Oils Magic: A Beginner's Guide to Working with Magical Oils, with Simple Recipes and Spells

Wicca Elemental Magic: A Guide to the Elements, Witchcraft, and Magical Spells

Wicca Magical Deities: A Guide to the Wiccan God and Goddess, and Choosing a Deity to Work Magic With

Wicca Living a Magical Life: A Guide to Initiation and Navigating Your Journey in the Craft

Magic and the Law of Attraction: A Witch's Guide to the Magic of Intention, Raising Your Frequency, and Building Your Reality

Wicca Altar and Tools: A Beginner's Guide to Wiccan Altars, Tools for Spellwork, and Casting the Circle

Wicca Finding Your Path: A Beginner's Guide to Wiccan Traditions, Solitary Practitioners, Eclectic Witches, Covens, and Circles

Wicca Book of Shadows: A Beginner's Guide to Keeping Your Own Book of Shadows and the History of Grimoires

Modern Witchcraft and Magic for Beginners: A Guide to Traditional and Contemporary Paths, with Magical Techniques for the Beginner Witch

FREE GIFT REMINDER

Just a reminder that Lisa is giving away an exclusive, free spell book as a thank-you gift to new readers!

Little Book of Spells contains ten spells that are ideal for newcomers to the practice of magic, but are also suitable for any level of experience.

Read it on read on your laptop, phone, tablet, Kindle or Nook device by visiting:

www.wiccaliving.com/bonus

DID YOU ENJOY *GREEN WITCHCRAFT FOR BEGINNERS*?

Thanks so much for reading this book! I know there are many great books out there about Wicca, so I really appreciate you choosing this one.

If you enjoyed the book, I have a small favor to ask—would you take a couple of minutes to leave a review for this book on Amazon?

Your feedback will help me to make improvements to this book, and to create even better ones in the future. It will also help me develop new ideas for books on other topics that might be of interest to you. Thanks in advance for your help!

www.ingramcontent.com/pod-product-compliance
Lightning Source LLC
Chambersburg PA
CBHW051729290426
43661CB00122B/119